T0294832

TIMING THE STOCK MARKET FOR MAXIMUM PROFITS

TIMING THE STOCK MARKET FOR MAXIMUM PROFITS

by Stanley S.C. Huang

WINDSOR BOOKS, BRIGHTWATERS, N.Y.

Published by Windsor Books
P.O. Box 280
Brightwaters, N.Y., 11718

Manufactured in the United States of America

ISBN 0-930233-16-6

CAVEAT: It should be noted that all trades, patterns, charts, systems, etc., discussed in this book are for illustrative purposes only and are not to be construed as specific advisory recommendations. Further note that no method of trading or investing is foolproof or without difficulty, and past performance is no guarantee of future performance. All ideas and material presented are entirely those of the author and do not necessarily reflect those of the publisher or bookseller.

Table of Contents

Publisher's Note

In order to make this book as timely and useful as possible, an update to Chapters 4, 5, 6, 7 and 8, is included at the end of each of those chapters. This updated material was provided by the author just prior to printing.

Chapter 1

The Technical Approach Is Often Misunderstood, Misstated And Misapplied

Technical analysis has been around for many, many years. Most investors have heard of it, and some of them are actually using it. Yet, technical analysis is the most debated subject among professors of finance and economics in the academic community and also on Wall Street.

Some people find technical analysis mysterious and are not convinced of its worth. Other people claim it means everything in investing and is far superior to fundamental analysis.

There are still others who stand between these two extreme positions. They find that technical analysis is useful in investing in some ways. They consider fundamental analysis equally, or more useful, than technical analysis. They find that each of the two approaches, technical and fundamental analysis, is particularly useful in certain aspects of investing.

There are many reasons why technical analysis is often misunderstood, misclaimed and misapplied. We will get into that after we first explain what technical analysis *really* is.

At this point, I would like to give you a little of my background and explain why I wrote this book. I have taught courses on investments in colleges for more than thirty years and have written several books on investing. I am now close to retirement and feel that there is a need to clear up the confusion about the subject matter of technical analysis. I do not have an ax to grind. I am not obligated to uphold certain pet theories of academicians or the "conventional wisdom." My purpose is simply to present an objective and dispassionate view of technical analysis. This book is designed to explain what technical analysis is, what it can and cannot do for investors, and how investors, both traders and non-traders, can benefit from understanding technical analysis.

Chapter 2

What Is Technical Analysis And Why Is It Often Misunderstood, Misstated And Misapplied?

WHAT IS TECHNICAL ANALYSIS?

Technical analysis is short-term market analysis. Short-term means a few days, weeks, or a few months. The stock and commodities markets can be analyzed in two ways:

One approach is to analyze the market changes and outlook through underlying economic and financial factors affecting demand and supply. In the stock market one would evaluate current business conditions, monetary policy, corporate earnings, profit margin, and expectation of inflation. The idea is to find out whether the current movements in stock prices will likely continue or tend to reverse. This approach can be properly labelled as short-term fundamental analysis.

The second approach is entirely different. It examines the market itself. It means looking at the changes in price and volume that are taking place in the market, as well as looking at associated factors such as market sentiment and the quality of trading in the market. This approach is known as technical analysis. The word "technical" is used to distinguish this type of analysis from fundamental analysis. The aim of this approach is not to inquire into the causes of market developments, but to *infer tendencies from market developments (transactions) themselves.*

The two approaches to short-term market analysis discussed above are not really mutually exclusive in the sense that one has to adopt either approach but not both. It is conceivable that some investors can skillfully use the two approaches at the same time. An example of this was the famous stock market forecaster, Edson Gould, who used the combined approach successfully for many years.

WHY ARE MOST ACADEMICIANS
AGAINST TECHNICAL ANALYSIS?

Most academicians are against technical analysis. Why? Could it be that technical analysis is really worthless as some academicians have argued? Or, is it due to the fact that academicians have failed to understand what technical analysis really is? Let us examine the question more thoroughly, because a correct understanding and evaluation of the criticisms of academicians to technical analysis can help us to formulate a correct view of technical analysis, and, therefore, to help make technical analysis more useful to investors.

The views of most academicians on investment in general and on technical analysis in particular can be discussed in terms of the following:

1) The assumption that investors are rational and risk averse
2) The theory of random walk
3) The theory of efficient market
4) Empirical evidence

Each of the above is explained briefly here:

1) *Assumption on the investment behavior of investors.* Many investment theories are formulated by academicians on the basis of the assumption that investors are rational in investment decisions and generally averse to risk. Other things being equal, they seek securities of maximum return when the risk is the same. Conversely, with a given level of return they seek securities of minimum risk.

2) *The theory of random walk.* Academicians believed that prices of securities are affected by news. Favorable news for the economy, industry, or a specific company will push stock prices up and unfavorable news will push prices down. The arrival of news, academicians believe, is of a "random walk" nature. This means good news, or bad, will arrive with total unpredictability.

3) *The theory of efficient market.* Academicians also believe that the financial markets in the U.S. are very efficient in the sense that:
   (a) News disseminates quickly among investors of all kinds.
   (b) Security prices adjust quickly to new information.

10

(c) No special group of investors has monopolistic access to important investment information; and no special group of investors has special influence on security prices.

(d) Security prices are accurate reflections of their "intrinsic value." The existence of thousands and thousands of financial analysts in the U.S. ensures that discrepancies between the value and the market prices of securities will not last long, primarily because this large number of analysts will detect and explore these discrepancies quickly.

4) *Empirical evidence.* Academicians are dedicated to the finding of truth. They always try to verify their theories with empirical evidence and vice versa, whenever possible.

Above, we have explained briefly the main tenets of academic views on investment. Now, we are in a position to cite the arguments many academicians make against technical analysis.

1) The most basic premise of technical analysis is the belief that stock prices tend to move in a trend. This premise is directly in conflict with the theory of random walk and the theory of efficient markets. Academicians argue that security prices fluctuate randomly in response to random arrival of news. They also charge that the trends in security prices the technicians may have found are trends in retrospect. The academicians also argue that since the financial markets are very efficient, any news of importance would be quickly reflected in the changes of prices of securities.

2) Academicians have employed various statistical methods to test whether there were dependencies or relations between successive prices of securities. They found none, or very little. To cite one study, Eugene Fama tested the independence of successive price changes by measuring serial correlations for the 30 industrial stocks in the Dow-Jones Industrial Index during a five-year period from 1957 to 1962. Table 2-1 shows the result of his correlation studies. In column 1 are the correlation coefficients between price changes of successive days for each stock in the DJIA. These coefficients are close to zero. The second column shows the correlation coefficients with a lag of two days. The results are similar. The other columns show correlation coefficients with a lag of three to ten days. The results are all close to zero, suggesting that there was only a negligible degree of relationship between successive price changes with a lag of one to ten days.

11

Table 2-1

Correlation Coefficients: Daily Price Changes versus Lagged Price Changes for
Each Dow Jones Industrial Company

	Lag in Days									
Stock	*1*	*2*	*3*	*4*	*5*	*6*	*7*	*8*	*9*	*10*
Allied Chemical	.02	−.04	.01	−.00	.03	.00	−.02	−.03	−.02	−.01
Alcoa	.12	.04	−.01	.02	−.02	.01	.02	.01	−.00	−.03
American Can	−.09	−.02	.03	−.07	−.02	−.01	.02	.03	−.05	−.04
AT&T	−.04	−.10	.00	.03	.01	−.01	.00	.03	−.01	.01
American Tobacco	.11	−.11	−.06	−.07	.01	−.01	.01	.05	.04	.04
Anaconda	.07	−.06	−.05	−.00	.00	−.04	.01	.02	−.01	−.06
Bethlehem Steel	.01	−.07	.01	.02	−.05	−.10	−.01	.00	−.00	−.02
Chrysler	.01	−.07	−.02	−.01	−.02	.01	.04	.06	−.04	.02
DuPont	.01	−.03	.06	.03	−.00	−.05	.02	.01	−.03	.00
Eastman Kodak	.03	.01	−.03	.01	−.02	.01	.01	.01	.01	.00
General Electric	.01	−.04	−.02	.03	−.00	.00	−.01	.01	−.00	.01
General Foods	.06	−.00	.05	.00	−.02	−.05	−.01	−.01	−.02	−.02
General Motors	−.00	−.06	−.04	−.01	−.04	−.01	.02	.01	−.02	.01
Goodyear	−.12	.02	−.04	.04	−.00	−.00	.04	.01	−.02	.01
Int'l. Harvester	−.02	−.03	−.03	.04	−.05	−.02	−.00	.00	−.05	−.02
Int'l. Nickel	.10	−.03	−.02	.02	.03	.06	−.04	−.01	−.02	.03
Int'l. Paper	.05	−.01	−.06	.05	.05	−.00	−.03	−.02	−.00	−.02
Johns Manville	.01	−.04	−.03	−.02	−.03	−.08	.04	.02	−.04	.03
Owens Illinois	−.02	−.08	−.05	.07	.09	−.04	.01	−.04	.07	−.04
Procter & Gamble	.10	−.01	−.01	.01	−.02	.02	.01	−.01	−.02	−.02
Sears	.10	.03	.03	.03	.01	−.05	−.01	−.01	−.01	−.01
Standard Oil (Cal.)	.03	−.03	−.05	−.03	−.05	−.03	−.01	.07	−.05	−.04
Standard Oil (N.J.)	.01	−.12	.02	.01	−.05	−.02	−.02	−.03	−.07	.08
Swift & Co.	−.00	−.02	−.01	.01	.06	.01	−.04	.01	.01	.00
Texaco	.09	−.05	−.02	−.02	−.02	−.01	.03	.03	−.01	.01
Union Carbide	.11	−.01	.04	.05	−.04	−.03	.00	−.01	−.05	−.04
United Aircraft	.01	−.03	−.02	−.05	−.07	−.05	.05	.04	.02	−.02
U.S. Steel	.04	−.07	.01	.01	.01	−.02	.04	.04	−.02	−.04
Westinghouse	−.03	−.02	−.04	−.00	.00	−.05	−.02	.01	−.01	.01
Woolworth	.03	−.02	.02	.01	.01	−.04	−.01	.00	−.09	−.01
Average	.03	−.04	−.01	.01	−.01	−.02	.00	.01	−.02	−.01

(Source: Eugene Fama, ''The Behavior of Stock Market Prices,'' *Journal of Business,* Jan. 1965.

EVALUATION OF THE ACADEMIC VIEWS
ON INVESTMENT AND TECHNICAL ANALYSIS

Assumption of Investment Behavior of Investors

It is reasonable to assume that investors in general are rational in investment decisions and risk averse. However, one should also bear in mind the following factors. First, greed and fear are also factors often entering into investment decisions. Second, from time to time investors are often swept into rampant enthusiasm or total despair. Many investors' behavior during these times can hardly be called rational. Third, investing deals with intangibles; the perception of future return and risk. There is no standard to go by.

The Theory of Random Walk

Academicians contend that the arrival of news is of a random nature. This is not necessarily true. We know that stock prices are one type of economic series, and that all economic series are affected by the business cycle. In a recovery phase of a business cycle, the news seems mostly favorable and good news can dominate for many months. Whereas in a recessionary period non-favorable news tends to dominate. When a company reports good news, it is more often than not followed up by more good news. The reverse happens to a company reporting bad news.

The Theory of Efficient Market

Most people would agree that the financial markets in the U.S. are by and large quite efficient. However, it is another matter to say that news is immediately reflected in changes in prices of securities. News is of all types. Some news, such as reporting of earnings and sales, is easy to interpret. Other news, such as change of management, merger, acquisition, new products, change of technology, new government regulation and so forth often requires special expertise to interpret, and can require significant amounts of time to investigate and to do an assessment of the impact it has had.

It is also a well documented fact that all investors do not have the same access to privileged information. Corporate insiders, specialists on the floor, and institutions with special contacts all have an advantage over other investors.

Empirical Evidence

There is a definite scarcity of information on investment performance using technical analysis. Investors who have successfully employed technical analysis often do not talk or write about their accomplishments. It would be foolish for them to reveal trade secrets, if they in fact know any.

While it is true that professors have found there to be little or no correlation between successive prices of securities, that does not prove that technical analysis is worthless. Far from it.

Technical analysis, correctly understood, is a short-term market analysis, analyzing the market itself; price and volume changes, the quality of trading and market sentiments. It is a composite, judgement approach, as is fundamental analysis. The only difference between the two approaches lies in *the factors being analyzed*: technical analysis looks at the market itself and fundamental analysis focuses on the underlying economic and financial factors.

WHERE IS THE TRUTH
ABOUT TECHNICAL ANALYSIS?

Simply put, the truth lies somewhere in between the position held by strong advocates of technical analysis and the position held by most academicians.

My view is as follows:

1) The basic premise of the technical analysis approach is that *stock prices move in a trend*. Edwards and Magee stated this premise in these words:

> "No one of experience doubts that prices move in trends, and trends tend to continue until something happens to change the supply-demand balance."

I feel the basic premise is only *partly true*. As correctly argued by academicians, the trends pointed out by advocates of technical analysis are usually the historical patterns of stock prices. They are usually trends "after the fact," not forecast in advance.

Oftentimes, stocks move sideways. At the beginning of a major move, upward or downward, nobody can tell that a major trend is in the making. It is typically only after the major trend has travelled some distance that technical analysts are in a position to say the trend is in existence. So the correct statement should be that stock prices move in a trend some of the time.

2) Technical analysis is a type of market analysis. A correctly performed market analysis of this type should reveal clues to the forthcoming movements of stock prices.

14

3) Technical analysis, if correctly done, should include momentum analysis of both price and volume. The concept of momentum applies to the physical world as well as to human affairs.

4) Stock prices are one type of economic time series. There are logical procedures to analyze changes in stock prices over time.

5) Technical analysis, if properly performed, in my view is as useful as fundamental analysis.

WHY IS TECHNICAL ANALYSIS OFTEN MISCLAIMED OR MISSTATED?

The reasons, as I see them, are these:

1) The usefulness of technical analysis is often misclaimed by special interest people. In order to sell more of their services to the public, some technical advisory services often exaggerate the usefulness of technical analysis as an investment tool and also exaggerate their own record of performance. Brokers' income depends on volume and the amount of customer transactions. The greater the volume of transactions, the greater is their income. Technical analysis tends to generate more transactions than does fundamental analysis, so you'll often find brokers steering their clients into more transactions through promoting and exaggerating the usefulness of technical analysis.

2) Some people have a habit of boasting about their abilities in just about everything and anything they do, including investing. They love to talk about their winners in the stock market, without mentioning any of their losers. They want to impress people by telling them how they used technical analysis to achieve their success.

3) Some people want to believe investing or trading is simple, and believe technical analysis proves their point.

4) Some people fail to understand what technical analysis really is. They think it is mechanical and that all it takes to succeed is to draw trend lines, support lines and resistance lines on charts of stocks (or stock indexes), to figure out what chart pattern the stock exhibits and then watch for the break-out or break-down signals. They fail to

15

understand that technical analysis is much more involved than that, and, moreover, that even a carefully performed technical analysis reveals only *probabilities.*

WHY IS TECHNICAL ANALYSIS OFTEN MISAPPLIED?

Technical analysis is often misapplied for various reasons. The most important reason is the fact that the user of this approach fails to understand fully what technical analysis really is and what it can and cannot do for the investor. To be specific, I will enumerate several common mistakes made by inexperienced followers of the technical approach:

1) They do not use stop-loss orders (orders instructing the broker to sell the stock when it reaches a certain price, usually below the current market price) in every transaction as a device to limit losses. As I have said, technical analysis, even if properly performed, reveals only *probabilities.* It is absolutely essential that the investor always use stop-loss orders to guard against big losses.

2) They are either timid or relatively inexperienced in selling short. The stock market fluctuates up, down, and sidewise. If one is inexperienced in short-selling, many opportunities which can be revealed by technical analysis will be passed up.

3) They often hesitate and move in only after prices have advanced or declined substantially. As a result, profits from correct moves are substantially reduced.

4) They fail to diversify and tend to use too much margin (borrowed money) relative to their own capital. As a consequence, they are often squeezed out of the market. Once out, it can be very difficult to return.

5) They trade too frequently and often take positions when they should stay on the sidelines. As a result, unnecessarily high commissions are paid out.

A RECENT EXAMPLE SHOWS WHY I SAY
TECHNICAL ANALYSIS IS A COMPOSITE JUDGEMENT APPROACH

In late March 1986 when the DJIA was around 1800, six leading technicians held a one-day seminar on the current state of the market. They were split on their market outlook and they differed on the factors they looked at and considered important.

One technician said he concentrated on the big picture and that the eighties may be a replay of the twenties.

The second technician felt that a correction of 5% to 10% was in the near term. However, the bull market had some time left, because the public was not yet heavily in. Major cyclical peaks were, in his view, at least several months away.

The third technician felt that the stock market was going through a classic blow-off period, citing the increasing sales of shares by financial corporations such as American Express and Morgan Stanley. He was very bearish.

The fourth technician was very, very bullish. He felt that the DJIA was going to keep rising until it reached about 3700 in 1988. He claimed that after it crossed 2000, the public would pour in.

The fifth technician felt that investors' psychology had become too bullish. He was also disturbed by the tremendous dichotomy between blue chips and secondaries. He was cautious on the near term market outlook.

The sixth technician saw a major top over the summer. He pointed out that the shorting by specialists was high and was a bearish sign.

From the above, we can see that these technicians differed sharply in their market outlook and they also differed on the factors they considered important at the moment. The factors mentioned by the technicians included stock market cycles, investors' sentiments, market trends, monetary conditions, patterns of individual stocks, public participation, short selling by specialists, and many others.

This current example confirms what was explained and emphasized before about the nature of technical analysis. In short, technical analysis is a type of short-term market analysis, analyzing the market itself.

Interpretations of the market depend on the factors examined, relative emphasis given to each factor, and the over-all judgement of the analyst himself. Technical analysis is far from mechanical. It is as much a judgement approach as is fundamental analysis.

TECHNICAL ANALYSIS, PROPERLY UNDERSTOOD & PERFORMED, CAN HELP ALL INVESTORS—TRADERS & NON-TRADERS

Technical analysis, if properly performed, can reveal important clues to future movement of the stock market and individual stocks. It is, therefore, very helpful to those investors who are interested in trading.

Some short-term traders do not rely totally on technical analysis for trading. They rely on technical analysis for market timing, but in the selection of individual securities, they rely on fundamental analysis.

Long-term investors should logically rely on fundamental analysis for selection of individual securities. However, in terms of timing of market trends, technical analysis can provide important clues to the status of the current market and its possible near-term trends. This type of input can help long-term investors select the optimal time to implement buy and sell decisions of individual securities. It is true, fundamental analysis can also be used to forecast the market. However, fundamental analysis is more conducive to long-term forecasting than short-term forecasting. Long-term investors stand to benefit by knowing both short-term and long-term possibilities of the market.

Chapter 3

The Dow Theory—A Forerunner of Modern-Day Technical Analysis

The Dow Theory is the foundation from which much of modern-day technical market analysis originates. The theory was formulated by Charles H. Dow and expressed in articles and editorials written by him for the Wall Street Journal around the turn of the 20th century. The theory was later interpreted, expanded, and refined by William P. Hamilton and Robert Rhea. The present day Dow theory is, therefore, a synthesis of the thoughts of Dow, Hamilton, and Rhea. The basic tenets of their theory are:

1) Dow's three movements
2) Determining the primary trend
3) Principle of confirmation
4) The "Line" formation
5) Relationship between volume and price movement

Dow's Three Movements

The "market," meaning the price of stocks in general, is always to be considered as having three movements, all going on at the same time. The first and the most important one is the primary trend, which is a broad upward or downward movement lasting usually a few years. The upward movement is also known as a bull market, and the downward movement as a bear market. The second movement represents intermediate reactions to the major trend, namely, important declines in a bull market or advances in a bear market. These interruptions in the major trend usually last several weeks to several months, retracing one-third to two-thirds of the price change in the preceding primary swing. The third movement represents day-to-day changes in security prices. Except as building blocks of the secondary movement, these daily fluctuations are not considered important by Dow theorists.

Determining the Primary Trend

A major upward trend is said to be in existence when successive rallies penetrate preceding high points with ensuing declines terminating above preceding low points. Conversely, a major downward movement is signified by successive rallies failing to reach preceding high points with ensuing declines carrying below preceding low points. In Figure 3-1 signals for bull and bear markets are indicated.

Figure 3-1

BULL AND BEAR MARKET SIGNALS

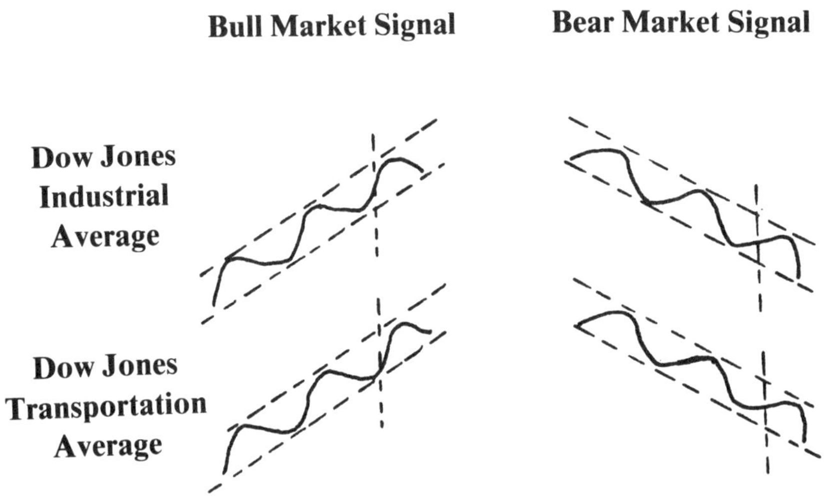

Bull Market Signal **Bear Market Signal**

**Dow Jones
Industrial
Average**

**Dow Jones
Transportation
Average**

20

Principles of Confirmation

A major upward movement found in the Dow-Jones Industrial Average does not automatically signal a bull market. For a bull market to come into existence, a similar upward movement has to be found also in the Dow Jones Transportation Average. Conversely, a bear market is signalled when both averages are found to be in a major downtrend movement. Should the Dow Jones Transportation Average fail to confirm the major movement of the Dow Jones Industrial Average, the current movement of the DJIA is considered suspect and the previous trend is considered still intact.

The "Line" Formation

A "Line" formation in Dow theory parlance represents a sidewise movement of several weeks' duration during which the price variations of both the Dow Jones Industrial and Transportation Averages move within a range of approximately 5%. The formation indicates that supply and demand are more or less in equilibrium. Simultaneous advances beyond the narrow range signify stronger forces of demand and predict higher prices, whereas simultaneous declines below the "Line" formation indicate lower prices to follow.

Relationship Between Volume and Price Movement

The Dow Theory as originally formulated by Charles H. Dow was based primarily on price movements of two Averages. However, Dow believed that volume pointed out the trend of prices. While William P. Hamilton rarely discussed the relation of volume to price movement, Robert Rhea stated clearly the relationship between the two. He said:

> A market which has been overbought becomes dull on rallies, and develops activity on declines; conversely, when a market is oversold, the tendency is to become dull on declines and active on rallies. Bull markets terminate in a period of excessive activity and begin with comparatively light transaction.

Nevertheless, volume in Dow Theory serves primarily as supporting evidence which may aid interpretation in practice. Trend signals are still dictated solely by changes in price movements.

DEFECTS OF THE DOW THEORY

We have explained the basic tenets of the Dow Theory; now we come to discuss its deficiencies and the criticisms made of it.

First, the theory is always late in identifying the major trend because of the requirement of seeing succeeding higher highs and higher lows to confirm bull markets (and conversely for bear markets); and the further requirement of confirmation between the two Averages.

Second, it is easy to identify in retrospect the intermediate price movements. However, it is rather difficult to differentiate the intermediate rallies and declines from the first stages of a bull or bear market while the price movements are in progress.

Third, the Dow Theory is designed to identify the major trend and, therefore, renders little help to the intermediate trend investor.

Fourth, the Dow Theory is based primarily on study of price movement. Volume data is not receiving sufficient attention.

DOW THEORY IN PRACTICE

The worth of a theory in the final analysis depends on the question of whether or not it works. Dr. Harvey A. Krow prepared a table (shown here as Table 3-1) on major movements in the stock market during 1897 - 1967 and the results which would have been achieved if the signals flashed by the Dow Theory were followed. (Please note that while the table has not been updated since 1967 it is still quite instructive for illustrating the value of the Dow Theory). The Dow confirmation signals shown in columns E and I were based on the principle of confirmation between Dow-Jones Industrial and Rail Averages, though the latter was not shown in the table. Column J shows the length of each major upward or downward move (column G minus C) in stock prices as registered in the Dow-Jones Industrial Average. Column K shows gains and losses (in parenthesis) if Dow signals were followed. Column L shows the percentage of the trend left from the confirmation at E until the ultimate high at G. The results as shown in the table can be summarized as follows:

1. The total profits in column K would amount to 1580 points, while losses came to 252.34, a ratio of six to one.

2. The Dow Theory follower can capture on the average 57.04 percent of all moves as shown in column L.

3. A comparison of columns J and K shows clearly that the Dow Theory is quite late in identifying the major trend.

Table 3-1
MAJOR MOVEMENTS IN THE STOCK MARKET 1897 - 1967

A Direction	B Start of Move Date	C (High)Low	D Dow Confirmation Date	E Price	F End of Move Date	G Price	H Dow Confirmation Date	I Price	J Total Move	K Dow Move (Loss)	L Percent After Dow Confirmation
1. Up	4/19/97	38.49	6/28/97	44.61	9/ 5/99	77.61	12/16/99	63.84	39.12	19.23	76.9
2. Down	9/ 5/99	(77.61)	12/16/99	63.84	6/23/00	53.68	10/20/00	59.44	-23.73	-4.40	42.7
3. Up	6/23/00	53.68	10/20/00	59.84	9/19/02	67.77	6/ 1/03	59.59	13.09	(-0.25)	60.5
4. Down	9/19/02	(67.77)	6/ 1/03	59.59	11/ 9/03	42.15	7/12/04	51.37	-27.62	-8.22	63.1
5. Up	11/ 9/03	42.15	7/12/04	51.37	1/19/06	103.00	4/26/06	92.44	60.85	41.07	84.9
6. Down	1/19/06	(103.00)	4/26/06	92.44	11/15/07	53.00	4/24/08	70.01	-50.00	-22.43	78.0
7. Up	11/15/07	53.00	4/24/08	70.01	11/19/09	100.53	5/ 3/10	84.72	47.53	14.71	64.2
8. Down	11/19/09	(100.53)	5/ 3/10	84.73	7/26/10	73.62	10/10/10	81.01	-26.91	-3.72	41.2
9. Up	7/26/10	73.62	10/10/10	81.01	7/30/12	94.15	1/14/13	84.96	20.53	3.95	64.0
10. Down	7/30/12	(94.15)	1/14/13	84.96	12/24/14	53.17	4/ 9/15	65.02	-40.96	-19.92	48.9
11. Up	12/24/14	53.17	4/ 9/15	65.02	12/21/16	110.15	8/28/17	86.12	56.98	21.10	52.4
12. Down	11/21/16	(110.15)	8/28/17	86.12	12/19/17	65.95	5/13/18	82.16	-44.20	-3.96	45.6
13. Up	12/19/17	65.95	5/13/18	82.16	11/ 3/19	119.62	2/ 5/20	99.96	53.97	17.80	69.4
14. Down	11/ 3/19	(119.62)	2/ 5/20	99.96	8/ 4/21	63.90	2/ 6/22	83.70	-55.72	-36.06	64.7
15. Up	8/ 4/21	63.90	2/ 6/22	83.70	10/14/22	103.43	6/20/23	90.81	39.53	7.11	49.9
16. Down	10/14/22	(103.43)	6/20/23	90.81	7/31/23	86.91	12/ 7/23	93.80	-16.52	(2.99)	23.6
17. Up	7/31/23	86.91	12/ 7/23	93.80	9/ 3/29	381.17	10/23/24	305.85	294.20	212.05	94.0
18. Down	9/ 3/29	(381.17)	10/23/29	305.85	7/ 8/32	41.22	7/24/33	84.29	-338.95	-221.56	78.0
19. Up	7/ 8/32	41.22	5/24/33	84.29	3/10/37	194.40	9/ 7/37	164.39	153.18	80.10	72.1
20. Down	3/10/37	(194.40)	9/ 7/37	164.39	3/31/38	98.95	6/23/38	127.40	-95.45	-36.99	68.6
21. Up	3/31/38	98.95	6/23/38	127.40	11/12/38	158.41	3/31/39	131.84	59.46	4.44	52.2

Table 3-1 (Cont'd)
MAJOR MOVEMENTS IN THE STOCK MARKET 1897 - 1967

A Direction	B Start of Move Date	C (High) Low	D Dow Confirmation Date	E Dow Confirmation Price	F End of Move Date	G Price	H Dow Confirmation Date	I Dow Confirmation Price	J Total Move	K Dow Move (Loss)	L Percent After Dow Confirmation
22. Down	11/12/38	(158.41)	3/31/39	131.84	4/ 8/39	121.44	7/17/39	142.58	-36.97	(10.74)	28.1
23. Up	4/ 8/39	121.44	7/17/39	142.58	9/12/39	155.92	5/13/40	137.63	34.48	(-4.95)	38.7
24. Down	9/12/39	(155.92)	5/13/40	137.63	4/28/42	92.92	6/15/44	145.86	-63.00	(8.23)	71.0
25. Up	4/28/42	92.92	6/15/44	145.86	5/29/46	212.50	8/27/46	191.04	119.58	45.18	55.7
26. Down	5/29/46	(212.50)	8/27/46	191.04	5/17/47	163.21	5/14/48	188.60	-49.29	-2.44	56.5
27. Up	5/17/47	163.21	5/14/48	188.60	6/15/48	193.16	11/ 9/48	173.94	29.95	(-14.66)	15.2
28. Down	6/15/48	(193.16)	11/ 9/48	173.94	6/13/49	161.60	10/ 2/50	228.94	-31.56	(55.00)	39.1
29. Up	6/13/49	161.60	10/ 2/50	228.94	1/ 5/53	293.79	8/31/53	261.22	132.19	32.28	49.1
30. Down	1/ 5/53	(293.79)	8/31/53	261.22	8/31/53	255.49	2/ 4/53	294.03	-38.30	(32.81)	15.0
31. Up	9/14/53	255.49	6/23/54	330.72	4/ 6/56	521.05	10/ 1/56	468.70	265.56	137.98	71.7
32. Down	4/ 6/56	(521.05)	10/ 1/56	468.70	10/22/57	419.79	5/ 2/58	459.56	-101.26	-9.14	48.3
33. Up	10/22/57	419.79	5/ 2/58	459.56	1/ 6/60	685.47	3/ 3/60	612.05	265.68	152.49	84.6
34. Down	1/ 6/60	(685.47)	3/ 3/60	612.05	10/26/60	566.05	10/10/61	706.87	-119.42	(94.82)	48.5
35. Up	10/26/60	566.05	10/10/61	706.87	12/13/61	734.91	4/26/62	678.88	168.86	(27.89)	16.6
36. Down	12/31/61	(134.91)	4/26/62	678.68	7/26/62	535.76	11/ 9/62	616.13	-195.15	-62.55	71.8
37. Up	7/26/62	535.76	11/ 9/62	616.13	2/ 9/66	995.15	5/ 5/66	899.77	459.39	281.64	61.1
38. Down	2/ 9/66	(995.15)	5/ 5/66	899.97	10/ 7/66	744.32	1/11/67	822.49	-250.83	-77.48	62.0
39. Up	10/ 7/66	744.32	1/11/67	822.49							

Source: Harvey A. Krow, Stock Market Behavior, The Technical Approach to Understanding Wall Street, pp. 42-43, Random House, New York, 1969.

4. The theory works well in major moves, but it is rather ineffective in minor moves as reflected in column K by the small losses incurred.

CONCLUSION

A few conclusions are now in order to indicate our views of the worth of the Dow Theory as a device to identify major trends in the stock market.

First, the Dow Theory correctly recognizes the importance of the concept of momentum underlying the movements of stock prices. Second, it is the originator of technical analysis. Much of modern day technical analysis originated from the concepts embodied in the Dow Theory. Third, the Dow Theory is a device for recognizing and following the major trend in stock prices. Though the signals are late, the approach can produce some profits in the long run. Fourth, while the theory is useful for earmarking major trends in movements of stock prices, investors and speculators alike should not expect to make good profits by relying only on this theory. The reason being that if the upward or downward moves signalled by the theory prove to be minor, losses will often arise due to frequent reversals in the marketplace.

Chapter 4

Identifying Market Trend With Moving Averages

In the previous chapter we explained the strength and weakness of the Dow Theory as a device to identify major trends in movements of stock prices. Economists, on the other hand, rely a great deal on a statistical method called a "moving average" in smoothing out a time series and in delineating a basic trend underlying the time series.

The procedure in the construction of a moving average for any series is relatively simple. First, we have to decide on the length of the moving average period. If we were to compute a 5-week moving average of a time series, we simply add up the first 5 weekly observations, then divide the sum by 5 to get a mean. This is the first moving average. To get the second moving average, we add the 6th observation to the total and subtract the very first item from the total, and then divide the new sum by 5. To get the third moving average we add the 7th item and subtract the 2nd item from the previous total to get a new total and a new average, and so on. The following table illustrates the moving average concept with a recent example, the calculation of a 5-week moving average of the DJIA for the first 10 weeks in 1984.

27

Table 4-1
CALCULATION OF A 5-WEEK MOVING AVERAGE
OF DOW-JONES INDUSTRIAL AVERAGE

End Of	DJIA	5-Week Moving Total		DJIA 5-Week Moving Average
1984				
1st. wk.	1286.6	—		—
2nd. wk.	1270.1	—		—
3rd. wk.	1259.1	—		—
4th. wk.	1239	—		—
5th. wk.	1197.1	6,242.9	(sum of wks. 1-5)	1248.6
6th. wk.	1160.7	6,117	(sum of wks. 2-6)	1223.4
7th. wk.	1148.9	5,995.8	(sum of wks. 3-7)	1199.2
8th. wk.	1165.1	5,901.8	(sum of wks. 4-8)	1180.4
9th. wk.	1171.5	5,843.3	(sum of wks. 5-9)	1168.7
10th. wk.	1139.8	5,786	(sum of wks. 6-10)	1157.2

The moving average line represents the basic trend of the time series which in this case are stock prices. Figure 4-1 below shows a hypothetical picture of weekly prices of DJIA with its 30 week moving average line.

Figure 4-1
A HYPOTHETICAL CHART OF WEEKLY CLOSING PRICES
OF THE DJIA AND ITS 30-WEEK MOVING AVERAGE

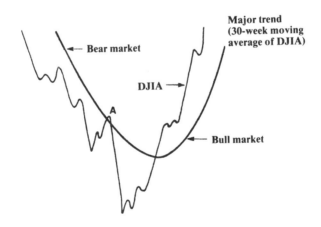

28

IDENTIFYING MAJOR TRENDS IN STOCK PRICES
BY A 30-WEEK MOVING AVERAGE

To identify major trends in stock prices, most analysts prefer either a 30-week or a 200-day moving average of a market index, such as the Standard & Poor's Index or the Dow-Jones Industrial Average. Since they produce about the same results, we prefer a 30-week moving average of the DJIA because of easier computations.

The interpretation of the moving average line is governed by two basic principles:

(1) A bull market (upward market) is believed to be in existence when the moving average line moves upward **and** the actual prices of the DJIA are above the moving average line.

(2) A bear market (downward market) is believed in existence when the moving average line is moving downward **and** the actual prices of the DJIA were below the moving average line.

In Figure 4-1, at point A the moving average line was descending, and the actual prices of the DJIA were above the moving average line. Since the moving average line represents the trendline, the trend at point A was still considered downward.

IDENTIFYING INTERMEDIATE OR SECONDARY TRENDS
BY 10-WEEK AND 20-WEEK MOVING AVERAGE OF DJIA

The moving average method can also be used for identification of intermediate or secondary trends in stock prices. Many traders are short-termed oriented. They are interested in changes of the overall stock market in the next few weeks or next couple of months.

In this respect, the statistical method of the moving average is superior to the Dow Theory, because the latter is aimed only at longer term major trends in stock prices. To identify intermediate trends, technical analysts use a variety of time periods: 10 days, 30 days, 45 days, 60 days, 10 weeks, 20 weeks, etc. *We prefer to identify the intermediate trend by taking both 10-week and 20-week moving averages of DJIA.* Our decision rules are:

1. The intermediate trend will most likely be upward if the 10-week moving average of the DJIA turns upward and, at the same time or in the following week, the 20-week moving average of the DJIA also turns upward.

2. The intermediate trend will most likely be downward if the 10-week moving

average of the DJIA turns downward and, at the same time or in the following week, the 20-week moving average of the DJIA also turns downward.

MOVING AVERAGE METHOD
TO IDENTIFY TRENDS IN PRACTICE

Table 4-2 shows DJIA and its 10-week, 20-week, and 30-week moving averages for the last 4½ years (Jan. 8, 1982 to June 13, 1986).

THE 30-WEEK MOVING AVERAGE
APPROACH PROVIDES THESE SIGNALS:

4-16-82	DJIA	843.2	M.A.	848.9	Turned upward
4-30-82	DJIA	848.4	M.A.	849.8	Turned downward
5-14-82	DJIA	857.8	M.A.	849.9	Turned upward
5-21-82	DJIA	835.9	M.A.	849.8	Turned downward

    Next low, DJIA   784.3
    Reached   8-6-82
    Difference from   5-21-82   Down 52 points

8-20-82   DJIA   869.3   M.A.   825.9   Turned upward
    Next high   1286.6
    Reached   1-7-84
    Difference from   8-20-82   Up 417 points

2- 3-84   DJIA 1197.1   M.A.   1235.5 Turned downward
    Next low   1086.9
    Reached   6-15-84
    Difference from   2-3-84   Down 110 points

8-25-84   DJIA 1236.5 M.A. 1152.8   Turned upward
    Latest DJIA in the table 1874.2
    Date: June 13, 1986
    Difference from   8-25-84   Up 638 points

(continued after Table 4-2)

Table 4-2
DOW JONES INDUSTRIAL AVERAGE AND ITS 10-WEEK, 20-WEEK,
& 30-WEEK MOVING AVERAGES 1982 - 1986

Date	DJIA	10-Wk. Mov.Av.	20-Wk. Mov. Av.	30-Wk. Mov.Av.
1-8-82	866.5	871.7	864	894.4
1-15	847.6	871.2	861.8	889.4
1-22	845	870.1	860.9	884.5
1-29	871.1	872 *	860.8	881.5
2-5	851	868.5 *	861.6 *	878.1
2-12	833.8	862.6	862.1	873.9
2-19	824.3	856.4	860.3 *	870.2
2-26	824.4	851.2	857.8	865.9
3-5	807.4	844.6	855.6	861.4
3-12	797.4	836.9	853.6	856.8
3-19	805.7	830.8	851.2	852.9
3-26	817.9	827.8	849.5	850.4
4-2	838.6	827.2	848.6	849.6
4-8	842.9	824.3	848.1	848.6
4-16	843.2	823.6	846	848.9 *
4-23	862.2	826.4 *	844.5	850.2
4-30	848.4	828.8	842.6	849.8 *
5-7	869.2	833.3	842.3	849.7
5-14	857.8	838.3	841.5	849.9 *
5-21	835.9	842.2	839.5	849.8 *
5-28	819.5	843.6	837.2	848.7
6-4	805	842.3 *	835	847.1
6-11	809.7	839.4	833.3	845.6
6-18	788.6	834	829.1	843.4
6-25	803.1	829.9	826.8	840.7
7-2	797	823.4	825	837.5
7-9	814.1	820	824.4	835.1
7-16	828.7	815.9	824.6 *	833.5
7-23	830.6	813.2	825.8	832.1
7-30	808.6	810.5	826.3	829.8
8-6	784.3	807	825.3 *	827.1
8-13	788.1	805.3	823.8	825.1
8-20	869.3	811.2 *	825.3 *	825.9 *
8-27	883.5	820.7	827.3	826.3
9-3	925.1	832.9	831.4	828.8
9-10	906.8	843.9	833.7	831.3
9-17	916.9	854.2	837.1	834.3
9-24	919.5	863.3	839.6	837.5
10-1	907.7	871	842.1	840.8
10-8	986.9	888.8	849.7	847.2
10-15	993.1	909.7	858.3	853.4
10-22	1031.5	934	869.7	860.5
10-29	991.7	946.3	878.8	865.7
11-5	1051.8	963.1	891.9	872.6
11-12	1039.9	974.6	903.8	879.2

* change of direction

Table 4-2 (Cont'd)

Date	DJIA	10-Wk. Mov. Av.	20-Wk. Mov. Av.	30-Wk. Mov. Av.
11-19	1021.3	986	915	884.5
11-26	1007.4	995.1	924.6	889.8
12-3	1031.4	1006.3	934.8	895.2
12-10	1018.8	1017.4	944.2	900.5
12-17	1011.5	1019.8	954.3	906.4
12-23	1045.1	1025	967.4	913.9
12-31	1046.5	1026.5	980.3	921.9
1-7-83	1076.1	1035	990.6	930.8
1-14	1080.9	1037.9	1000.5	940.6
1-21	1053	1039.2	1006.9	948.9
1-28	1064.8	1043.6	1014.8	957.8
2-4	1077.9	1050.6	1022.8	966.6
2-11	1086.5	1056.1	1031.2	975.2
2-18	1092.8	1063.5	1040.4	983.9
2-25	1120.9	1074.5	1047.1	994.3
3-4	1141	1084	1054.5	1006.2
3-11	1117.7	1091.2	1058.9	1017.2
3-18	1117.7	1095.3	1065.2	1025.6
3-25	1140.1	1101.2	1069.6	1034.1
3-31	1130	1108.9	1074.1	1040.9
4-8	1124.7	1114.9	1079.2	1048.1
4-15	1171.3	1124.3	1087.4	1056.7
4-22	1196.3	1135.3	1095.7	1065.9
4-29	1226.2	1148.6	1106.1	1076.5
5-6	1232.6	1159.8	1117.1	1084.7
5-13	1218.8	1167.5	1125.8	1092.2
5-20	1190	1174.8	1133	1097.5
5-27	1216.1	1184.6	1140	1105
6-3	1213	1191.9	1146.6	1110.4
6-10	1196.1	1198.5	1153.7	1115.5
6-17	1242.2	1210.3	1162.6	1122.9
6-24	1241.7	1217.3	1170.8	1130.7
7-1	1225.3	1220.2	1177.7	1137.2
7-8	1207.2	1218.3 *	1183.4	1143.4
7-15	1192.3	1214.3	1187	1149.5
7-22	1231	1215.5 *	1191.5	1155.7
7-29	1199.2	1216.4	1195.6	1160.8
8-5	1183	1213.1 *	1198.9	1164.4
8-12	1182.8	1210.1	1201	1167.7
8-19	1194.2	1209.9	1204.2	1172.4
8-26	1192.1	1204.9	1207.6	1176.7
9-2	1215.4	1202.2	1209.8	1181.3
9-9	1239.7	1203.7 *	1211.9	1186.4
9-16	1225.7	1205.5	1211.9	1190.8
9-23	1255.5	1211.9	1213.1	1195.1
9-30	1233.1	1212.1	1213.8	1198.2
10-7	1272.1	1219.4	1217.9	1203.4
10-14	1263.5	1227.4	1220.2	1208.2
10-21	1248.8	1234	1222	1211.9
10-28	1223.5	1236.9	1223.4	1215

* change of direction

32

Table 4-2 (Cont'd)

Date	DJIA	10-Wk. Mov. Av.	20-Wk. Mov. Av.	30-Wk. Mov. Av.
11-3	1218.3	1239.6	1222.2 *	1218.1
11-10	1250.2	1243	1222.6 *	1220.7
11-17	1251.1	1244.2	1223.9	1222.5
11-24	1277.4	1249.4	1227.4	1224.3
12-2	1265.3	1250.3	1231.1	1225.3
12-9	1260.1	1253	1232.5	1226.7
12-17	1242.1	1250 *	1234.7	1228.5
12-24	1250.5	1248.7	1238.1	1229.6
12-30	1258.6	1249.7*	1241.9	1231.1
1-7-84	1286.6	1256	1246.5	1234.1
1-14	1270.1	1261.2	1250.4	1235.1
1-21	1259.1	1262.1	1252.6	1235.7
1-27	1230	1260 *	1252.1 *	1235.8
2-3	1197.1	1251.9	1250.6	1235.5 *
2-10	1160.7	1241.5	1245.9	1234.4
2-17	1148.9	1230.4	1241.7	1231.7
2-24	1165.1	1222.7	1236.3	1230.6
3-2	1171.5	1214.8	1231.7	1230.2
3-9	1139.8	1202.9	1226.3	1228.7
3-16	1184.3	1192.7	1224.3	1228.4
3-23	1154.8	1181.1	1221.1	1227.3
3-30	1164.9	1171.7	1216.9	1225.6
4-6	1132.2	1161.9	1211	1222
4-13	1150.1	1157.2	1204.6	1219.5
4-20	1158.1	1157	1199.2	1216.3
4-27	1169.1	1159 *	1194.7	1214.1
5-4	1165.3	1159	1190.8	1210.6
5-11	1157.1	1157.6 *	1186.2	1207
5-18	1133.8	1157	1179.9	1203.2
5-25	1107.1	1149.3	1170.9	1199.3
6-1	1124.4	1146.2	1163.7	1196.2
6-8	1131.3	1142.9	1157.3	1192.2
6-15	1086.9	1138.3	1150.1	1186.7
6-22	1131.1	1136.4	1146.8	1181.8
6-29	1132.4	1133.9	1145.4	1177.4
7-6	1122.6	1129.2	1144.1	1172.9
7-13	1109.9	1123.7	1141.3	1168.4
7-20	1101.4	1118.1	1137.8	1163.5
7-24	1114.6	1116.2	1136.6	1158.7
8-3	1202.1	1125.7 *	1137.5 *	1155.9
8-10	1218.1	1135	1140.6	1154.1
8-17	1211.9	1143.1	1143	1152.6
8-25	1236.5	1158.1	1148.2	1152.8 *
8-31	1224.4	1167.4	1151.9	1153.7
9-7	1207.4	1174.9	1154.4	1155.3

* change of direction

33

Table 4-2 (Cont'd)

Date	DJIA	10-Wk. Mov. Av.	20-Wk. Mov. Av.	30-Wk. Mov. Av.
9-14-84	1237.5	1186.4	1157.8	1158.2
9-21	1201.7	1195.6	1159.7	1159.4
9-28	1206.7	1206.1	1162.1	1160.6
10-5	1182.5	1212.9	1164.6	1162.0
10-12	1190.7	1211.7 *	1168.7	1162.2
10-19	1225.9	1212.5 *	1173.8	1164.6
10-26	1205.0	1211.8 *	1177.5	1165.9
11-2	1216.7	1209.9	1184.0	1168.8
11-9	1219.0	1209.3	1188.4	1171.0
11-16	1187.9	1207.4	1191.2	1172.1
11-23	1220.3	1205.6	1196.0	1173.7
11-30	1188.9	1204.4	1200.0	1174.6
12-7	1163.2	1200.0	1203.1	1174.7
12-14	1175.9	1199.4	1206.2	1176.2
12-21	1199.0	1200.2 *	1206.0 *	1179.2
12-28	1204.2	1198.0 *	1205.3	1181.9
1-4-85	1185.0	1196.0	1203.9	1183.7
1-11	1218.1	1196.2 *	1203.1	1188.1
1-18	1227.4	1197.0	1203.2 *	1191.3
1-25	1276.1	1205.8	1206.6	1196.1
2-1	1277.7	1211.6	1208.6	1201.2
2-8	1290.0	1221.7	1213.1	1207.2
2-15	1282.0	1233.5	1216.8	1213.2
2-22	1275.8	1243.5	1221.5	1218.6
3-1	1299.4	1253.6	1226.9	1221.9
3-8	1269.7	1260.1	1229.1	1223.6
3-15	1247.4	1266.4	1231.2	1224.7
3-22	1267.5	1271.3	1233.8	1225.8
3-29	1266.8	1275.2	1236.1	1227.2
4-4	1259.0	1273.5 *	1239.7	1228.9
4-12	1265.7	1272.3	1242.0	1229.8
4-19	1266.6	1270.0	1245.9	1232.1
4-26	1275.2	1269.3	1251.4	1234.3
5-3	1274.2	1266.5	1255.0	1236.5
5-10	1274.2	1263.9	1258.8	1239.2
5-17	1285.3	1265.5 *	1262.8	1241.2
5-24	1302.0	1271.0	1268.7	1244.5
5-31	1315.4	1275.7	1273.5	1274.8
6-7	1316.4	1280.7	1278.0	1251.0
6-14	1301.0	1284.9	1279.2	1254.8
6-21	1324.5	1290.8	1281.6	1258.3
6-28	1335.5	1297.7	1283.9	1263.2
7-5	1334.5	1303.6	1286.5	1268.8
7-12	1338.6	1312.7	1289.6	1274.2
7-19	1359.5	1321.3	1292.6	1279.6
7-26	1357.1	1328.5	1297.0	1284.7
8-2	1353.0	1333.6	1302.3	1290.3
8-9	1320.8	1334.1	1304.9	1293.7
8-16	1312.7	1333.7 *	1307.2	1296.6
8-23	1318.3	1335.5 *	1310.2	1298.0
8-30	1334.0	1336.4	1313.6	1299.9

* change of direction

34

Table 4-2 (Cont'd)

Date	DJIA	10-Wk. Mov. Av.	20-Wk. Mov. Av.	30-Wk. Mov. Av.
9-6-85	1335.7	1336.4	1317.1	1301.4
9-13	1307.7	1333.7 *	1318.7	1302.2
9-20	1297.9	1329.7	1321.2	1303.0
9-26	1320.8	1325.8	1323.6	1303.7
10-4	1328.7	1323.0	1325.8	1305.7
10-11	1339.9	1321.7	1327.7	1308.8
10-18	1368.8	1326.5 *	1330.3	1312.1
10-25	1356.5	1330.8	1332.3	1315.1
11-1	1390.3	1338.0	1336.8	1319.5
11-8	1404.4	1345.1	1340.8	1324.1
11-15	1435.1	1355.0	1345.7	1329.7
11-22	1464.3	1370.7	1352.2	1336.0
11-29	1472.1	1388.1	1358.9	1343.5
12-6	1477.2	1403.7	1364.8	1350.3
12-13	1535.2	1424.4	1373.7	1358.7
12-20	1543.0	1444.7	1383.2	1366.7
12-27	1543.0	1462.1	1394.3	1374.2
1-3-86	1549.2	1481.4	1406.1	1382.0
1-10	1513.5	1493.7	1415.9	1389.1
1-17	1536.7	1506.9	1426.0	1396.2
1-24	1529.9	1516.4	1435.7	1402.6
1-31	1571.0	1527.1	1448.9	1410.5
2-7	1613.4	1541.2	1464.7	1419.7
2-14	1664.5	1559.9	1481.8	1429.8
2-21	1697.7	1576.2	1500.3	1441.2
2-28	1709.1	1592.8	1518.8	1453.1
3-7	1699.8	1608.5	1535.3	1465.7
3-14	1792.7	1632.8	1557.1	1481.7
3-21	1768.6	1658.3	1576.0	1496.7
3-27	1821.7	1686.8	1596.9	1512.9
4-4	1739.2	1707.8	1612.1	1526.4
4-11	1790.2	1729.7	1628.4	1542.5
4-18	1840.4	1752.4	1646.8	1560.6
4-25	1835.6	1769.5	1664.7	1577.7
5-2	1774.7	1777.2	1676.7	1592.6
5-9	1789.4	1785.2	1689.0	1607.6
5-16	1759.8	1791.2	1699.9	1620.6
5-23	1823.3	1794.3	1713.6	1636.2
5-30	1876.7	1805.1	1731.7	1652.4
6-6	1885.9	1811.5	1749.2	1668.4
6-13	1874.2	1825.0	1766.4	1683.1

* change of direction

The results of the 30-week approach can be summarized as follows:

1. Three signals given in April and May, 1982 were misleading.
2. The signal on May 21, 1982 was correct, but the subsequent move was a minor one.
3. The signal on August 20, 1982 was correct, and the subsequent move was very big.
4. The signal on Feb. 3, 1984 was correct, and the subsequent move was relatively moderate.
5. The signal on Aug. 25, 1984 was correct, and the subsequent move up to June 13, 1986 was tremendous.

10-WEEK AND 20-WEEK CONFIRMATION APPROACH

Now we turn to *identifying the intermediate trend* using the approach we preferred. That is the approach requiring a confirmation of both 10-week and 20-week moving averages within one week's time to validate a signal.

The 10-week and 20-week confirmation approach provided these signals:

10-Week M.A. Signal	20-Week M.A. Confirmed
8-20-82	8-20-82
DJIA 869.3 M.A. 811.2 turn upward	M.A. 825.3 turn upward
Next high	1286.6
Reached	1-7-84
Difference from 8-20-82	up 417 points
1-27-84	1-27-84
DJIA 1230 M.A. 1260 turn downward	M.A. 1252.1 turn downward
Next low	1086.9
Reached	6-15-84
Difference from 1-27-84	143 points lower
8-3-84	8-3-84
DJIA 1202.1 M.A. 1125.7 turn upward	M.A. 1137.5 turn upward
Next high	1237.5
Reached	9-14-84
Difference from 8-3-84	up 35 points

```
12-28-84                                    12-21-84
DJIA  1204.2  M.A.  1198  turn downward          M.A.  1206  turn downward
                    Next high          1185
                    Reached            1-4-85
                    Difference from 12-28-84    19 points lower

1-11-85                                     1-18-85
 DJIA  1218.1  M.A.  1196.2  turn upward          M.A.  1203.2  turn upward
                    Latest DJIA in the table    1874.2
                    Date:  June 13, 1986
                    Difference from 1-11-85     up 656 points
```

The results of the 10-week and 20-week confirmation approach were:

1. The signal on 8-10-82 was correct, and the subsequent move was very big.

2. The signal on 1-27-84 was correct, and the subsequent move was of moderate size.

3. The signal on 8-3-84 was correct, but yielded only 35 points.

4. The signal on 12-28-84 was correct, but was reversed two weeks later.

5. The signal on 1-11-85 was a genuine signal and provided 656 points up to June 13, 1986.

The comparison of results between the 30-week approach and the 10-week/20-week confirmation approach yielded the following:

1. The 10-week/20-week confirmation approach did not flash misleading signals as the 30-week approach did in the Spring of 1982.

2. The 30-week approach flashed a bullish signal on 8-25-84 and remained so up to June 13, 1986.

3. The 10-week/20-week confirmation approach flashed a bullish signal earlier on 8-3-84, but changed its signal later on 12-28-84. It moved back to a bullish stand on 1-11-85 and stayed the same up to June 13, 1986.

4. For this 4½ year period, from January 1982 to June 1986, the two approaches seemed to provide comparable results.

5. For intermediate-term traders, the 10-week/20-week confirmation approach provides more flexibility and more occasions for switching.

UPDATE—RECENT DEVELOPMENTS DURING THE PERIOD FROM JUNE 13, 1986 TO FEB 13, 1987

This manuscript was completed in June 1986. The weekly ending price recorded for DJIA in Table 4-2 was 1874.2 on June 13, 1986. In order to provide up to date information to my readers, I've prepared a supplement to Table 4-2 showing the developments in the stock market during the seven months from June 13, 1986 to Feb. 13, 1987.

The 30-Week Moving Average Approach

The 30-week moving average approach provided these signals:

10- 3-86	DJIA	1774.2	30-wk. M.A.	1814.0	turn downward
10-10-86	DJIA	1793.2	30-wk. M.A.	1820.1	turn upward

The signal given on Oct. 3, 1986 was misleading. It was reversed in the following week. That means that the upward trend was still intact.

The 10-Week and 20-Week Confirmation Approach

The 10-week and 20-week confirmation approach provided these signals:

10-Week M.A. Signal	**20-Week M.A. Confirmed**
8-22-86	8-22-86
DJIA 1887.8 M.A. 1836.5 turn upward	M.A. 1830.8 turn upward
Next high	1899.8
Reached	9-5-86
Difference from 8-22-86	up 12 points
9-12-86	9-12-86
DJIA 1758.7 M.A. 1825.6 turn downward	M.A. 1835.3 turn downward
Next low	1762.7
Reached	9-19-86
Difference from 9-12-86	up 4 points
11-21-86	11-28-86
DJIA 1893.6 M.A. 1830.1 turn upward	M.A. 1832.5 turn upward
Latest DJIA in the table	2183.3
Difference from 11-21-86	up 289.7 points

The results of the 10-week and 20-week confirmation approach can be summarized as follows:

1. The signal on 8-22-86 was not meaningful. It yielded only 12 points.
2. The signal on 9-12-86 was not correct. It yielded a negative result of 4 points.

Table 4-2 Supplement
DJIA AND ITS 10-WEEK, 20-WEEK
& 30-WEEK MOVING AVERAGES 1986-1987

Date	DJIA	10-Wk. Mov. Av.	20-Wk. Mov. Av.	30-Wk. Mov. Av.
6-20-86	1879.5	1834	1781.9	1696.9
6-27	1885.3	1838.4	1795.4	1710.7
7-3	1900.9	1845	1807.3	1724.8
7-11	1821.4	1849.6	1813.4	1734.3
7-18	1778.0	1848.5*	1816.9	1742.2
7-25	1810.0	1853.5*	1813.4*	1751.1
8-1	1763.6	1847.6*	1821 *	1758.3
8-8	1782.6	1838.1	1821.6	1767.2
8-15	1855.6	1835.1	1823.3	1777.8
8-22	1887.8	1836.5*	1830.8	1789.8
8-29	1898.3	1838.4	1836.2	1800.7
9-5	1899.8	1839.8	1839.1	1810.2
9-12	1758.7	1825.6*	1835.3*	1813.4
9-19	1762.7	1819.7	1834.7	1815.5
9-26	1769.7	1818.9	1833.7	1817.6
10-3	1774.2	1815.3	1834.4*	1814.0*
10-10	1793.2	1818.3*	1833 *	1820.1*
10-17	1837.0	1823.7	1830.9	1822.3
10-23	1832.3	1821.4*	1828.3	1822.7
10-31	1877.8	1820.4	1828.5*	1827.3
11-7	1886.5	1819.2	1828.8	1830.5
11-14	1873.6	1816.6	1828.2*	1831.6
11-21	1893.6	1830.1*	1827.9	1833.6
11-28	1914.2	1845.2	1832.5*	1838.2
12-7	1925.0	1860.7	1839.8	1842.7
12-14	1912.2	1874.5	1844.9	1847.8
12-20	1928.9	1888.1	1853.2	1851.4
12-26	1930.4	1897.5	1860.6	1853.1
1-2-87	1927.3	1907	1864.2	1854.5
1-9	2005.9	1919.8	1870.1	1858.9
1-16	2076.6	1938.8	1879	1865.5
1-23	2101.5	1961.6	1889.1	1872.7
1-30	2158	1988.0	1909.1	1881.3
2-6	2186.8	2015.3	1930.3	1893.4
2-13	2183.3	2041.1	1950.9	1906.9

* **change of direction**

39

3. When there are frequent reversals in the 10-week moving average or 20-week moving average, or both, the market trend is basically indeterminate. The signals given by the confirmation approach under these circumstances didn't yield good results, as shown in the above two signals.

4. The signal on 11-28-86 was a genuine signal and provided 290 points so far.

CONCLUSION

1. When the market trend is indeterminate, as shown by the 10-week and 20-week confirmation approach, the 30-week moving average can provide some clue as to the future trend in stock prices.

2. The signals given by the 10-week and 20-week confirmation approach should not be implemented when there are frequent reversals in the 10-week moving average, 20-week moving average, or both. The potential is limited.

3. The 10-week and 20-week confirmation approach is a useful approach. When the signal given by the confirmation approach is in line with the 30-week approach, the potential can be great as shown in the latest signal given on 11-21-86.

Chapter 5

Measuring Momentum Of Market Trend

Many followers of technical analysis believe that once a trend is established, upward or downward, it tends to continue forward until a new balance of supply and demand emerges.

The best way to gauge the strength or momentum of a trend is to find out the speed, or rate of change, of its movement. As shown in Table 5-1, the procedure we follow in the computation of rates of changes in stock prices requires these steps:

1. Compute a percentage change of price between the current weekly closing price of DJIA and that of 5 weeks ago.

2. Take a 5-week moving average of the rates of change derived under step (1).

3. Also take a 10-week moving average of the rates of change derived under step (1).

The second and third steps are designed to smooth out random changes and to show the basic trend in the rates of change of stock prices. The 5-week moving average shows the immediate trend which is subject to frequent reversals, whereas the 10-week moving average shows the long-term trend which is less volatile and, therefore, more reliable.

PRINCIPLES OF INTERPRETATION

The principles of interpretation of the computed rates of changes of stock price are as follows:

A. A bullish signal is given when two conditions are met:

(continued after Table 5-1)

Table 5-1
RATE OF CHANGE ANALYSIS OF STOCK PRICE
January 1982 - June 1986

Date	DJIA	% Change From 5 Wks. Ago	5-Wk. Mov.Av.	Indicator (Signal)	Evaluation Of Record	10-Wk. Mov.Av.	Indicator (Signal)	Evaluation Of Record
1-8-82	866.5	–	–			–		
1-15	847.6	–	–			–		
1-22	845	–	–			–		
1-29	871.1	–	–			–		
2-5	851	–	–			–		
2-12	833.8	-3.78	–			–		
2-19	824.3	-2.75	–			–		
2-26	824.4	-2.44	–			–		
3-5	807.4	-7.31	–			–		
3-12	797.4	-6.30	-4.52			–		
3-19	805.7	-3.37	-4.43			–		
3-26	817.9	-0.78	-4.04			–		
4-2	838.6	1.72	-3.21			–		
4-8	842.9	4.40	-0.87	Bullish	Poor	–		
4-16	843.2	5.74	1.54			-1.49		
4-23	862.2	7.01	3.62			-0.41	Bullish	Poor
4-30	848.4	3.73	4.52			0.24		
5-7	869.2	3.65	4.91			0.85		
5-14	857.8	1.77	4.38			1.76		
5-21	835.9	-0.86	3.06			2.30		
5-28	819.5	-4.95	0.67	Bearish	Poor	2.14		
6-4	805	-5.11	-1.10			1.71		
6-11	809.7	-6.85	-3.20			0.85	Bearish	Poor
6-18	788.6	-8.07	-5.17			-0.39		
6-25	803.1	-3.92	-5.78			-1.36		
7-2	797	-2.75	-5.34			-2.34		
7-9	814.1	1.13	-4.09			-2.60		
7-16	828.7	2.35	-2.25			-2.73		
7-23	830.6	5.33	0.43	Bullish	Excellent	-2.37		
7-30	808.6	0.68	1.35			-2.22		
8-6	784.3	-1.59	1.58			-1.88		
8-13	788.1	-3.19	0.72			-1.69		
8-20	869.3	4.90	1.23			-0.51	Bullish	Excellent
8-27	883.5	6.37	1.43			0.93		
9-3	925.1	14.41	4.18			2.76		
9-10	906.8	15.62	7.62			.4.60		
9-17	916.9	16.34	11.53			6.12		
9-24	919.5	5.77	11.70			6.46		
10-1	907.7	2.74	10.98			6.21		
10-8	986.9	6.68	9.43			6.81		
10-15	993.1	9.52	8.21			7.92		
10-22	1031.5	12.50	7.44			9.49		
10-29	991.7	7.85	7.86			9.78		

Table 5-1 (Cont'd)

Date	DJIA	% Change From 5 Wks. Ago	5-Wk. Mov. Av.	Indicator (Signal)	Evaluation Of Record	10-Wk. Mov. Av.	Indicator (Signal)	Evaluation Of Record
11-5	1051.8	15.88	10.49			10.73		
11-12	1039.9	5.37	10.22			9.83		
11-19	1021.3	2.84	8.89			8.55		
11-26	1007.4	-2.34	5.92			6.68		
12-3	1031.4	4.00	5.15			6.50		
12-10	1018.8	-3.14	1.35			5.92		
12-17	1011.5	-2.73	-0.27			4.98		
12-23	1045.1	2.33	-0.38			4.26		
12-31	1046.5	3.88	0.87			3.39		
1-7-83	1076.1	4.33	0.93			3.04		
1-14	1080.9	6.10	2.78			2.06		
1-21	1053.0	4.10	4.15			1.94		
1-28	1064.8	1.88	4.06			1.84		
2-4	1077.9	3.00	3.88			2.38		
2-11	1086.5	0.97	3.21			2.07		
2-18	1092.8	1.10	2.21			2.50		
2-25	1120.9	6.45	2.68			3.41		
3-4	1141.0	7.16	3.74			3.90		
3-11	1117.7	3.69	3.87			3.88		
3-18	1117.7	2.87	4.25			3.73		
3-25	1140.1	4.33	4.90			3.56		
3-31	1130.0	0.81	3.77			3.23		
4-8	1124.7	-1.43	2.05			2.90		
4-15	1171.3	4.80	2.28			3.08		
4-22	1196.3	7.03	3.11			3.68		
4-29	1226.2	7.55	3.75			4.33		
5-6	1232.6	9.08	5.41			4.59		
5-13	1218.8	8.37	7.37			4.71		
5-20	1190.0	1.60	6.73			4.50		
5-27	1216.1	1.66	5.65			4.38		
6-3	1213.0	-1.08	3.93			3.84		
6-10	1196.1	-2.96	1.52			3.46		
6-17	1242.2	1.92	0.23			3.80		
6-24	1241.7	4.34	0.78			3.75		
7-1	1225.3	0.76	0.60			3.12		
7-8	1207.2	-0.48	0.72			2.32		
7-15	1192.3	-0.32	1.24			1.38		
7-22	1231.0	-0.90	0.68	Bearish	Neutral	0.45	Bearish	Neutral
7-29	1199.2	-3.42	-0.87			-0.05		
8-5	1183.0	-3.45	-1.71			-0.56		
8-12	1182.8	-2.02	-2.02			-0.65		
8-19	1194.2	0.16	-1.93			-0.34		
8-26	1192.1	-3.16	-2.38			-0.85		
9-2	1215.4	1.35	-1.42			-1.15		
9-9	1239.7	4.79	0.22	Bullish	Fair	-0.75		
9-16	1225.7	3.63	1.35			-0.33	Bullish	Fair
9-23	1255.5	5.13	2.35			0.21		
9-30	1233.1	3.44	3.67			0.64		

43

Table 5-1 (Cont'd)

Date	DJIA	% Change From 5 Wks. Ago	5-Wk. Mov.Av.	Indicator (Signal)	Evaluation Of Record	10-Wk. Mov.Av.	Indicator (Signal)	Evaluation Of Record
10-7	1272.1	4.66	4.33			1.45		
10-14	1263.5	1.92	3.75			1.99		
10-21	1248.8	1.88	3.41			2.38		
10-28	1223.5	-2.55	1.87			2.11		
11-3	1218.3	-1.20	0.94	Bearish		2.31		
11-10	1250.2	-1.72	-0.33			2.00		
11-17	1251.1	-0.98	-0.91			1.42		
11-24	1277.4	2.29	-0.83	Bullish		1.29		
12-2	1265.2	3.41	0.36			1.12		
12-9	1260.1	3.43	1.29			1.11		
12-17	1242.1	-0.65	1.50			0.58		
12-24	1250.5	-0.05	1.69			0.39		
12-30	1258.6	-1.47	0.93	Bearish		0.05		
1-7-84	1286.6	1.69	0.59	Bullish		0.48		
1-14	1270.1	0.79	0.06			0.67		
1-21	1259.1	1.37	0.47			0.98		
1-27	1230.0	-1.64	0.15	Bearish	Fair	0.92		
2-3	1197.1	-4.89	-0.54			0.20	Bearish	Fair
2-10	1160.7	-9.79	-2.83			-1.12		
2-17	1148.9	-9.54	-4.90			-2.42		
2-24	1165.1	-7.47	-6.67			-3.10		
3-2	1171.5	-4.76	-7.29			-3.57		
3-9	1139.8	-4.79	-7.27			-3.90		
3-16	1184.3	2.03	-4.91			-3.87		
3-23	1154.8	0.51	-2.90			-3.90		
3-30	1164.9	-0.02	-1.41			-4.04		
4-6	1132.2	-3.35	-1.12			-4.21		
4-13	1150.1	0.90	0.01	Bullish		-3.63		
4-20	1158.1	-2.21	-0.83	Bearish		-2.87		
4-27	1169.1	1.24	-0.69	Bullish		-1.79		
5-4	1165.3	0.03	-0.68			-1.04		
5-11	1157.1	2.20	0.43			-0.35		
5-18	1133.8	-1.42	-0.03	Bearish		-0.01		
5-25	1107.1	-4-40	-0.47			-0.65		
6-1	1124.4	-3.82	-1.48			-1.09		
6-8	1131.3	-2.92	-2.07			-1.38		
6-15	1086.9	-6.07	-3.73			-1.65		
6-22	1131.1	-0.24	-3.49			-1.76		
6-29	1132.4	2.29	-2.15			-1.31		
7-6	1122.6	-0.16	-1.42			-1.45		
7-13	1109.9	-1.89	-1.21			-1.64		
7-20	1101.4	1.33	0.27	Bullish		-1.73		
7-27	1114.6	-1.46	0.02	Bearish		-1.73		
8-3	1202.1	6.16	0.80	Bullish		-0.68	Bullish	
8-10	1218.1	8.51	2.53			0.56		
8-17	1211.9	9.19	4.75			1.77		
8-25	1236.5	12.27	6.93			3.60		
8-31	1224.4	9.85	9.20			4.61		
9-7	1207.4	0.44	8.05			4.42		

Table 5-1 (Cont'd)

Date	DJIA	% Change From 5 Wks. Ago	5-Wk. Mov.Av.	Indicator (Signal)	Evaluation Of Record	10-Wk. Mov.Av.	Indicator (Signal)	Evaluation Of Record
9-14	1237.5	1.59	6.67			4.60		
9-21	1201.7	-0.84	4.66			4.71		
9-28	1206.7	-2.41	1.73			4.33		
10-5	1182.5	-3.42	-0.93	Bearish		4.14		
10-12	1190.7	-1.38	-1.29			3.38		
10-19	1225.9	-0.94	-1.80			2.44		
10-26	1205.0	0.27	-1.58			1.54		
11-2	1216.7	0.83	-0.93	Bullish		0.40		
11-9	1219.0	3.09	0.37			-0.28		
11-16	1187.9	-0.24	0.60	Bearish	Neutral	-0.35	Bearish	Neutral
11-23	1220.3	-0.46	0.70			-0.55		
11-30	1188.9	-1.34	0.38			-0.60		
12-7	1163.2	-4.40	-0.67			-0.80		
12-14	1175.9	-3.54	-2.00			-0.82		
12-21	1199.0	0.93	-1.76			-0.58	Bullish	
12-28	1204.2	-1.32	-1.93			-0.62	Bearish	
1-4-85	1185.0	-0.33	-1.73			-0.68		
1-11	1218.1	4.74	0.10	Bullish	Fair	-0.29	Bullish	Fair
1-18	1227.4	4.38	1.68			-0.16		
1-25	1276.1	6.43	2.78			0.51		
2-1	1277.7	6.11	4.27			1.17		
2-8	1290.0	8.86	6.10			2.19		
2-15	1282.0	5.25	6.21			3.16		
2-22	1275.8	3.94	6.12			3.90		
3-1	1299.4	1.83	5.20			3.99		
3-8	1269.7	-0.63	3.85			4.06		
3-15	1274.4	-3.30	1.42			3.76		
3-22	1276.5	-1.13	0.14	Bearish		3.18		
3-29	1266.8	-0.71	-0.79			2.67		
4-4	1259.0	-3.11	-1.78			1.71		
4-12	1265.7	-0.32	-1.71			1.07		
4-19	1266.6	1.54	-0.75	Bullish		0.34		
4-26	1275.2	0.61	-0.40			-0.13		
5-3	1247.2	-1.55	-0.57	Bearish		-0.68	Bearish	
5-10	1274.2	1.21	0.30	Bullish	Fair	-0.74	Bullish	Fair
5-17	1285.3	1.55	0.67			-0.52		
5-24	1302.0	2.79	0.92			0.09		
5-31	1315.4	3.15	1.43			0.52		
6-7	1316.4	5.55	2.85			1.14		
6-14	1301.0	2.10	3.03			1.67		
6-21	1324.5	3.05	3.33			2.00		
6-28	1335.5	2.57	3.28			2.10		
7-5	1334.5	1.45	2.94			2.19		
7-12	1338.6	1.69	2.17			2.51		
7-19	1359.5	4.50	2.65			2.84		
7-26	1357.1	2.46	2.53			2.93		
8-2	1353.0	1.31	2.28			2.78		
8-9	1320.8	-1.03	1.79			2.37		
8-16	1312.7	-1.93	1.06			1.62		

45

Table 5-1 (Cont'd)

Date	DJIA	% Change From 5 Wks. Ago	5-Wk. Mov.Av.	Indicator (Signal)	Evaluation Of Record	10-Wk. Mov.Av.	Indicator (Signal)	Evaluation Of Record
8-23	1318.3	-3.03	-0.44	Bearish	Neutral	1.11		
8-30	1334.0	-1.70	-1.28			0.63	Bearish	Neutral
9-6	1335.7	-1.58	-1.79			0.25		
9-13	1307.7	-0.99	-1.79			0		
9-20	1297.9	-1.13	-1.63			-0.29		
9-26	1320.8	0.19	-0.98	Bullish		-0.71	Bullish	
10-4	1328.7	-0.40	-0.72	Bearish		-1.00	Bearish	
10-11	1339.9	0.37	-0.39	Bullish	Excellent	-1.09		
10-18	1368.8	4.67	0.74			-0.53	Bullish	Excellent
10-25	1356.5	4.51	1.87			0.12		
11-1	1390.3	5.26	2.88			0.95		
11-8	1404.4	5.70	4.10			1.69		
11-15	1435.1	7.11	5.45			2.53		
11-22	1464.3	6.98	5.91			3.33		
11-29	1472.1	8.52	6.71			4.29		
12-6	1477.2	6.25	6.91			4.90		
12-13	1535.2	9.31	7.63			5.87		
12-20	1543.0	7.52	7.72			6.59		
12-27	1543.0	5.37	7.39			6.65		
1-3-86	1549.2	5.24	6.74			6.72		
1-10	1513.5	2.46	5.98			6.45		
1-17	1536.7	0.10	4.14			5.89		
1-24	1529.9	-0.85	2.46			5.09		
1-31	1571.0	1.81	1.75			4.57		
2-7	1613.4	4.14	1.53			4.14		
2-14	1664.5	9.98	3.04			4.51		
2-21	1697.7	10.48	5.11			4.63		
2-28	1709.1	11.71	7.62			5.04		
3-7	1699.8	8.20	8.90			5.33		
3-14	1792.7	11.11	10.30			5.92		
3-21	1768.6	6.25	9.55			6.30		
3-27	1821.7	7.30	8.91			7.01		
4-4	1739.2	1.76	6.92			7.27		
4-11	1790.2	5.32	6.35			7.63		
4-18	1840.4	2.66	4.66			7.48		
4-25	1835.6	3.79	4.17			6.86		
5-2	1774.7	-2.58	2.19			5.55		
5-9	1789.4	2.89	2.42			4.67		
5-16	1759.8	-1.70	1.01			3.68		
5-23	1823.3	-0.93	0.29	Bearish		2.48		
5-30	1876.7	2.24	-0.02	Bullish		2.08		
6-6	1885.9	6.27	1.75			1.97		
6-13	1874.2	4.74	2.12			2.27		

46

1) The rate of decline in the 5-week moving average was diminished to a level less than 1%, and

2) The current rate of change of stock price against 5 weeks ago has already turned into a positive figure.

B. A bearish signal is given when two conditions are met:

1) The rate of increase in the 5-week moving average has dropped to a level less than 1%, and

2) The current rate of change of stock prices against 5 weeks ago has already turned to a negative figure.

C. When bearish signals are followed by bullish signals (and vise-versa) within a period of 3 weeks, the market trend is sidewise and indeterminate.

D. When indicators of 5 and 10-week moving averages confirm each other, the trend indicated in most cases will be reliable.

REVIEW OF RECORD

In Table 5-1, we show the weekly closing prices of the DJIA, their rates of change, bullish and bearish signals, and an evaluation of their performance for the period from January 1982 to June 1986.

The 5 and 10-week moving averages confirmed each other and provided 15 signals during the period as shown below:

Confirmed Signals During the Period
From Jan. 1982 to June 1986

Date	DJIA	Confirmed Indicator	Performance
4-23-82	862.2	Bullish	Poor
6-11-82	809.7	Bearish	Poor
8-20-82	869.3	Bullish	Excellent
7-22-83	1231.0	Bearish	Neutral
9-16-83	1225.7	Bullish	Fair
2- 3-84	1197.1	Bearish	Fair
8- 3-84	1202.1	Bullish	Neutral
11-16-84	1187.9	Bearish	Neutral
1-11-85	1218.1	Bullish	Fair
5- 3-85	1247.2	Bearish	Followed by reversal a week later
5-10-85	1274.2	Bullish	Fair
8-30-85	1334.0	Bearish	Neutral
9-26-85	1320.8	Bullish	Followed by reversal a week later
10- 4-85	1328.7	Bearish	Followed by reversal 2 weeks later
10-18-85	1368.8	Bullish	Excellent (500 points up as of 6-13-86)

47

Three out of the 15 signals were followed by reversals within two weeks. The performance of the remaining 12 signals was: 2 poor, 4 neutral, 4 fair, and 2 excellent. The important point, however, is that during the period there were two major upward moves and our confirmation signal approach did capture both of them.

The rate of change analysis discussed here provides the short-term investor (trader) with a good view of the momentum of the market and can be extremely helpful in finding out whether the current trend is sidewise, levelling off, accelerating or reversing. Our recommended procedure of waiting for confirmation by both 5 and 10-week moving averages of the rates of change enabled the speculator to capture the big moves and to receive fair results on the minor move in the stock trend. There were only two bad calls, and they caused only minor losses.

We feel that the advance and decline data analyzed in the way just suggested will provide the short-term trader with a useful indicator of the future market trend.

UPDATE—RECENT DEVELOPMENTS IN THE STOCK MARKET DURING THE PERIOD FROM JUNE 13, 1986 TO FEB. 13, 1987

To bring our readers up to date on developments in the stock market during the seven months from June 1986 to Feb. 1987, I've prepared a supplement to Table 5-1 on rates of change in stock prices.

The 5 and 10-week moving averages confirmed each other and provided 4 signals during the latest seven month period as shown below:

Date	DJIA	Confirmed Indicator	Performance
7-18-86	1778	Bearish	Poor
8-29-86	1898.3	Bullish	Followed by reversal in 3 wks.
9-26-86	1769.7	Bearish	Poor
10-31-86	1877.8	Bullish	Excellent

One signal was followed by a reversal in 3 weeks. Two other signals were poor, but yielded only moderate losses. The latest signal, however, was excellent. It was given on 10-31-86 when the DJIA was 1877.8. So far it has yielded 305 points. This bullish signal was given 3 weeks earlier than that given by the 10-week and 20-week confirmation approach discussed in the previous chapter.

This recent experience indicated again that the rate of change approach is a useful indicator. It is more sensitive than the 10-week and 20-week confirmation approach.

Table 5-1 Supplement

RATE OF CHANGE ANALYSIS OF STOCK PRICES (1986 - 1987)

Date	DJIA	% Change From 5 Wks. Ago	5-Wk. Mov. Av.	Indicator (Signal)	Evaluation Of Record	10-Wk. Mov.Av.	Indicator (Signal)	Evaluation Of Record
6-20-86	1879.5	6.80	3.82			2.09		
6-27	1885.3	3.40	4.69			2.12		
7-3	1900.9	1.29	4.50			1.99		
7-11	1821.4	-3.42	2.56			1.51		
7-18	1778.0	-5.13	0.59	Bearish	Poor	0.83	Bearish	Poor
7-25	1810.0	-3.70	-1.51			0		
8-1	1763.6	-6.46	-3.48			-0.89		
8-8	1782.6	-6.22	-4.99			-1.64		
8-15	1855.6	1.88	-3.93			-1.35		
8-22	1887.8	6.18	-1.66			-0.54	Bullish	Neutral
8-29	1898.3	4.88	0.05	Bullish	Poor	-0.73		
9-5	1899.8	7.72	2.89			-0.30		
9-12	1758.7	-1.34	3.86			-0.56	Bearish	Neutral
9-19	1762.7	-5.00	2.49			-0.72		
9-26	1769.7	-6.26	0	Bearish	Poor	-0.83		
10-3	1774.2	-6.54	-2.28			-1.12		
10-10	1793.2	-5.61	-4.95			-1.03		
10-17	1837.0	4.45	-3.79			0.04	Bullish	Excellent
10-23	1832.3	3.95	-2.00			0.24		
10-31	1877.8	6.11	0.47	Bullish	Excellent	0.24		
11-7	1886.5	6.33	3.05			0.38		
11-14	1873.6	4.48	5.06			0.06		
11-21	1893.6	3.08	4.79			0.50		
11-28	1914.2	4.47	4.89			1.45		
12-7	1925.0	2.51	4.17			2.32		
12-14	1912.2	1.36	3.18			3.12		
12-20	1928.9	2.95	2.87			3.97		
12-26	1930.4	1.94	2.65			3.72		
1-2-87	1927.3	0.68	1.89			3.39		
1-9	2005.9	4.20	2.23			3.20		
1-16	2076.6	8.60	3.67			3.43		
1-23	2101.5	8.95	4.87			3.87		
1-30	2158	11.79	6.84			4.75		
2-6	2186.8	13.46	9.40			5.65		
2-13	2183.3	8.84	10.33			6.28		

Diffusion Index Of Advancing and Declining Issues On New York Stock Exchange Can Confirm and Predict Market Trend

Through the use of the confirmed moving average method, we know what the current trend is. The rate of change analysis just discussed tells us the momentum of the current trend. However, we do not know how widespread the current trend is among individual issues. The diffusion index is designed to reveal how individual issues participate in the current trend in stock prices.

The diffusion index is a statistical series indicating the percentage of items in a group which is rising at any given time. As shown in the accompanying Table 6-1, the construction of the diffusion index is relatively simple. First, we combine the number of weekly advances and declines on the New York Stock Exchange; then we divide the number of advances by the total number of advancing and declining issues to get a percent of issues advanced. In order to smooth out erratic changes so as to discover the trend move easily, we finally take a 3-week moving average of the percent of issues advanced.

Table 6-1
DIFFUSION INDEX OF ADVANCING ISSUES ON NYSE

Week Ending	DJIA	Weekly Advances	Weekly Declines	Total Issues	% of Issues Advanced	3-Week Mov. Av.
1- 3-86	1549.2	1333	629	1962	67.9	—
1-10-86	1513.5	767	1310	2077	36.9	—
1-17-86	1536.7	1382	624	2006	68.9	57.9
1-24-86	1529.9	908	1082	1990	45.6	50.5
1-31-86	1571	1377	661	2038	67.6	60.7
2- 7-86	1613.4	1330	706	2036	65.3	59.5
2-14-86	1664.5	1490	560	2050	72.7	68.5
2-21-86	1697.7	1502	519	2021	74.3	70.8

The diffusion index as a statistical tool has an interesting quality, that is, it tends to change direction ahead of the aggregate as shown in Figure 6-1. When the diffusion index starts to descend from a high level, the aggregate will continue to ascend. Conversely, when the diffusion index begins to rise from a low level, the aggregate will continue to decline. Only after the diffusion index rises to the 50 percent line will the aggregate cease to decrease. In other words, the diffusion index, if correctly interpreted, will have predictive value of the probable forthcoming change in the aggregate.

Figure 6-1 below is a hypothetical case in which we show the normal relationship between the Diffusion Index of advancing issues on NYSE and a market index of stock prices.

Figure 6-1
THE NORMAL RELATIONSHIP BETWEEN
MARKET INDEX OF STOCK PRICES AND
THE DIFFUSION INDEX OF ADVANCING ISSUES ON NYSE

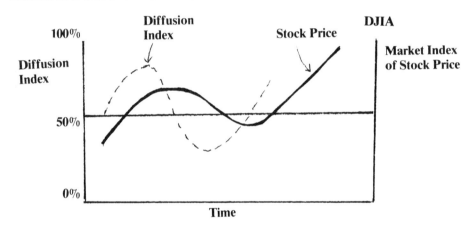

INTERPRETATION OF THE DIFFUSION INDEX

After the computation of the diffusion index is completed in a table, the data on the index should be charted. The diffusion index line in a chart should be interpreted in three ways:

a) Observe the direction of movement of the diffusion index line: upward, downward or sidewise.
b) Compare its direction of movement with that of the Dow-Jones Industrial Average.
c) See whether the diffusion index line is above or below the 50% neutral line.

The direction of movement of the diffusion index line should receive the closest attention. Because of the nature of the construction of the diffusion index, the diffusion index will change direction earlier than the general market index, such as the DJIA or the Standard & Poor's Index. In general, a rising diffusion index line is bullish and a falling line is bearish.

A comparison between the movements of the DJIA and the diffusion index line will indicate whether the prevailing trends in stock prices will continue. When a rising DJIA is accompanied by a rising diffusion index, the prevailing bullish trends will likely continue. However, when there is a disparity between the movements of the DJIA and the diffusion index, the direction of the latter usually foretells the former.

In general, when the level of the diffusion index is lower than 45% it is bearish. Conversely, when its level is higher than 55%, it is bullish. However, when interpreting the diffusion index, one should be concerned with its level as well as its direction of movement. *In general, the direction of movement of the diffusion index should receive more weight than its absolute level.* For example, a rising diffusion index beyond the 50% line should be considered very bullish. A rising line in the area of 40 to 50%, on the other hand, is only moderately bullish. A rising line in the area of 30 to 40% can only be labelled as neutral. Conversely, a falling line of the diffusion index above the 50% neutral line will indicate that the present bullish trend in stock prices may not hold for long. A falling line below the 50% neutral line will indicate either an impending market decline or a signal that the current decline will probably last for a while.

RECORD OF PERFORMANCE

Now we can turn to an examination of the record of performance of the diffusion index in the last 4½ years. Table 6-2 shows the statistics on the diffusion index together with weekly closing prices of the DJIA for the period January 1982 to June 1986. The same data is charted in Figure 6-2. Examination of the data yields these findings:

1. The diffusion index reached a low in early June 1982 and then turned around and moved up. It reached a peak in early Sept. 1982. The DJIA reached a low in early August 1982 and then turned around and moved up, reaching a peak for the year in early Nov. 1982. The diffusion index led the DJIA by about two months.

2. The diffusion index was above 50%, but fluctuated within a range of 50% to 70% for the first half of 1983, and then in July 1983 it went down sharply, suggesting that the upward move of the DJIA may soon end and can turn downward.

(continued after Table 6-2)

53

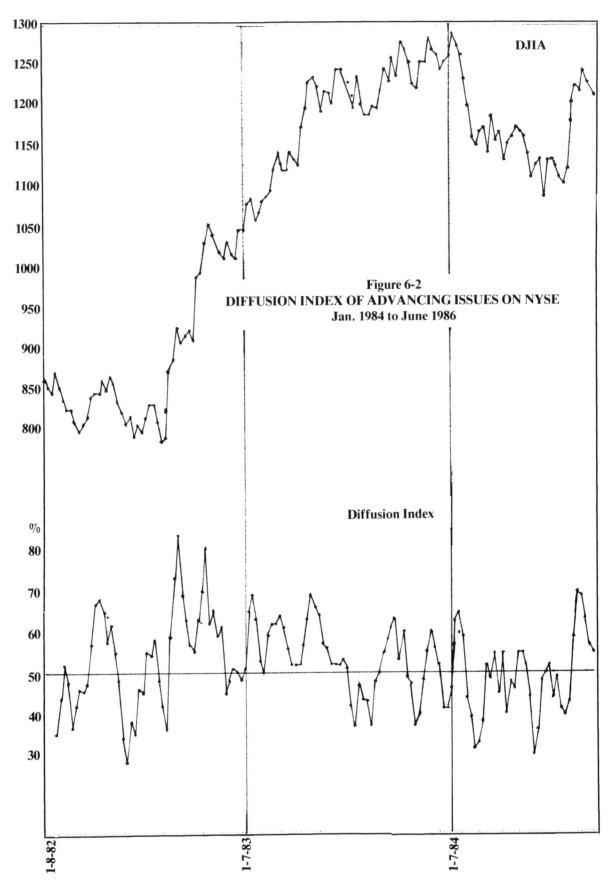

DJIA

Figure 6-2
DIFFUSION INDEX OF ADVANCING ISSUES ON NYSE
Jan. 1984 to June 1986

Diffusion Index

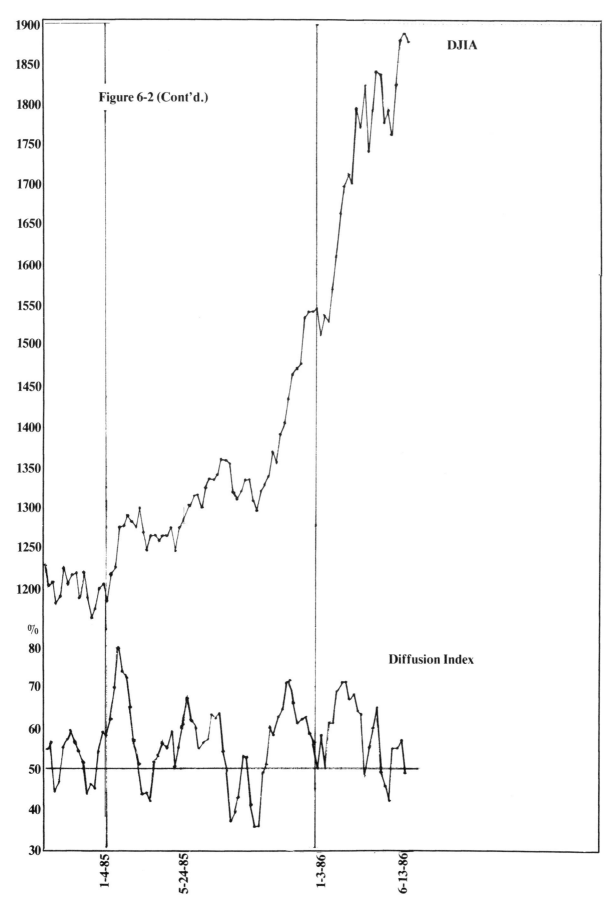

DJIA

Figure 6-2 (Cont'd.)

Diffusion Index

%

1-4-85   5-24-85   1-3-86   6-13-86

Table 6-2
DIFFUSION INDEX OF ADVANCING ISSUES ON NYSE
Jan. 1982 to Sept. 1984

Week Ending	DJIA	Weekly Advances	Weekly Declines	% Advanced	3-Week Mov.Av.
1-8-82	866.5	832	1086	43.4	–
1-15	847.6	406	1489	21.4L	–
1-22	845	735	1083	40.4	35.1
1-29	871.1	1361	543	71.5	44.4
2-5	851	818	1061	43.5	51.8
2-12	833.8	520	1349	27.8	47.6
2-19	824.3	739	1050	41.3	37.5
2-26	824.4	1059	836	55.9	41.7
3-5	807.4	779	1162	40.1	45.8
3-12	797.4	751	1119	40.2	45.4
3-19	805.7	1134	709	61.5	47.3
3-26	817.9	1292	565	69.6	57.1
4-2	838.6	1288	559	69.7	66.9
4-8	842.9	1155	650	64	67.8
4-16	643.2	1139	749	60.3	64.7
4-23	862.2	1253	622	66.8	63.7
4-30	848.4	857	1047	45	57.4
5-7	869.2	1388	509	73.2	61.7
5-14	857.8	885	985	47.3	55.2
5-21	835.9	428	1454	22.7	47.7
5-28	819.5	578	1289	31	33.7
6-4	805	563	1258	30.9	28.2L
6-11	809.7	947	920	50.7	37.5
6-18	788.6	441	1436	23.5	35.0
6-25	803.1	1148	683	62.7	45.6
7-2	797	881	951	48.1	44.8
7-9	814.1	941	833	53	54.6
7-16	828.7	1109	720	60.6	53.9
7-23	830.6	1097	727	60.1	57.9
7-30	808.6	447	1433	23.8	48.2
8-6	784.3	736	1082	40.5	41.5
8-13	788.1	816	1042	43.9	36.1
8-20	869.3	1866	180	91.2H	58.5
8-27	883.5	1653	345	82.7	72.6
9-3	925.1	1500	446	77.1	83.7H
9-10	906.8	899	966	48.2	69.3
9-17	916.9	1214	692	63.7	63.0
9-24	919.5	1095	792	58	56.6
10-1	907.7	822	1044	44.1	55.3
10-8	986.9	1739	263	86.9	63.0
10-15	993.1	1620	417	79.5	70.2
10-22	1031.5	1546	458	77.1	81.2
10-29	991.7	600	1369	30.5	62.4
11-5	1051.8	1381	221	89.2	65.6
11-12	1039.9	1131	864	56.7	58.8

Table 6-2 (Cont'd)

Week Ending	DJIA	Weekly Advances	Weekly Declines	% Advanced	3-Week Mov.Av.
11-19	1021.3	740	1206	38	61.3
11-26	1007.4	749	1149	39.5	44.7
12-3	1031.4	1240	725	63.1	46.9
12-10	1018.8	986	957	50.7	51.1
12-17	1011.5	702	1265	35.7	49.8
12-23	1045.1	1098	814	57.4	47.9
12-31	1046.5	1158	771	60	51.0
1-7-83	1076.1	1536	463	76.8	64.7
1-14	1080.9	1386	624	69	68.6
1-21	1053.0	829	1144	42	62.6
1-28	1064.8	958	1014	48.6	53.2
2-4	1077.9	1183	768	60.6	50.4
2-11	1086.5	1360	615	68.9	59.4
2-18	1092.8	1097	856	56.2	61.9
2-25	1120.9	1163	790	59.5	61.5
3-4	1141.0	1548	466	76.9	64.2
3-11	1117.7	913	1052	46.5	61.0
3-18	1117.7	874	1053	45.4	56.3
3-25	1140.1	1253	704	64	52.0
3-31	1130.0	874	1016	46.2	51.9
4-8	1124.7	899	1053	46.1	52.1
4-15	1171.3	1588	420	79.1H	57.1
4-22	1196.3	1297	709	64.7	63.3
4-29	1226.2	1255	736	63	68.9H
5-6	1232.6	1427	607	70.2	66
5-13	1218.8	1203	833	59.1	64.1
5-20	1190	821	1174	41.2	56.8
5-27	1216.1	1368	644	68	56.1
6-3	1213	914	1055	46.4	51.9
6-10	1196.1	866	1144	43.1	52.5
6-17	1242.2	1334	682	66.2	51.9
6-24	1241.7	1015	1019	50	53.1
7-1	1225.3	728	1278	36.3	50.8
7-8	1207.2	760	1189	39	41.8
7-15	1192.3	699	1299	35	36.8L
7-22	1231	1313	665	66.4	46.8
7-29	1199.2	580	1426	28.9L	43.4
8-5	1183	671	1322	33.7	43
8-12	1182.8	939	1009	48.2	36.9
8-19	1194.2	1225	743	62.2	48.0
8-26	1192.1	781	1163	40.2	50.2
9-2	1215.4	1255	711	63.8	55.4
9-9	1239.7	1331	609	68.6	57.5
9-16	1225.7	977	985	49.8	60.7
9-23	1255.5	1420	604	70.2	62.9
9-30	1233.1	786	1169	40.2	53.4

Table 6-2 (Cont'd)

Week Ending	DJIA	Weekly Advances	Weekly Declines	% Advanced	3-Week Mov.Av.
10-7	1272.1	1412	630	69.1	59.8
10-14	1263.5	769	1211	38.8	49.4
10-21	1248.8	652	1326	33.0	47
10-28	1223.5	739	1222	37.7	36.5
11-3	1218.3	939	1013	48.1	39.6
11-10	1250.2	1172	810	59.1	48.3
11-17	1251.1	1157	839	58.0	55.1
11-24	1277.4	1218	763	61.5	59.5
12-2	1265.2	963	1052	47.8	55.8
12-9	1260.1	901	1097	45.1	51.5
12-17	1242.1	622	1414	30.6	41.2
12-24	1250.5	925	1086	46.0	40.6
12-30	1258.6	1212	767	61.2	45.9
1-7-84	1286.6	1678	388	81.2H	62.8
1-14	1270.1	1066	983	52	64.8H
1-21	1259.1	925	1130	45	59.4
1-27	1230.0	737	1300	36.2	44.4
2-3	1197.1	713	1327	35	38.7
2-10	1160.7	480	1607	23	31.4
2-17	1148.9	820	1169	41.2	33.1
2-24	1165.1	982	917	50.1	38.1
3-2	1171.5	1307	683	65.7	52.3
3-9	1139.8	603	1413	29.9	48.6
3-16	1184.3	1394	579	70.7	55.4
3-23	1154.8	670	1305	33.9	44.8
3-30	1164.9	1179	786	60	54.9
4-6	1132.2	546	1494	26.8	40.2
4-13	1150.1	1143	854	57.2	48.0
4-20	1158.1	1037	890	53.8	45.9
4-27	1169.1	1056	917	53.5	54.8
5-4	1165.3	1168	800	59.3	55.5
5-11	1157.1	852	1140	42.8	51.9
5-18	1133.8	579	1415	29.0	43.7
5-25	1107.1	402	1634	19.7L	30.5L
6-1	1124.4	1151	781	59.6	36.1
6-8	1131.3	1320	690	65.7	48.3
6-15	1086.9	507	1473	25.6	50.3
6-22	1131.1	1294	699	64.9	52.1
6-29	1132.4	830	1120	42.6	44.4
7-6	1122.6	765	1129	40.4	49.3
7-13	1109.9	784	1189	39.7	40.9
7-20	1101.4	750	1210	38.3	39.5
7-27	1114.6	1013	981	50.8	42.9
8-3	1202.1	1838	267	87.3	58.8
8-10	1218.1	1481	593	71.4	69.8
8-17	1211.9	952	1022	48.2	69.0
8-25	1236.5	1414	613	69.8	63.1
8-31	1224.4	1026	907	53.1	57.0
9-7	1207.4	791	1139	41.0	54.6

H: High for the year   L: Low for the year

Table 6-2 (Cont'd)

Week Ending	DJIA	Weekly Advances	Weekly Declines	% Advanced	3-Week Mov.Av.
9-14	1237.5	1411	584	70.7	54.9
9-21	1201.7	1041	986	51.4	54.4
9-28	1206.7	939	1054	47.1	56.4
10-5	1182.5	668	1312	33.7	44.1
10-12	1190.7	1158	809	58.9	46.6
10-19	1225.9	1518	563	72.9	55.2
10-26	1205.0	796	1223	39.4	57.1
11-2	1216.7	1294	703	64.8	59.0
11-9	1219.0	1295	702	64.8	56.3
11-16	1187.9	629	1375	31.4	53.7
11-23	1220.3	1140	796	58.9	51.7
11-30	1188.9	789	1198	39.7	43.3
12-7	1163.2	801	1206	39.9	46.2
12-14	1175.9	1080	914	54.2	44.6
12-21	1199.0	1343	663	66.9	53.7
12-28	1204.2	1063	819	56.5	59.2
1-4-85	1185.0	961	934	50.7	58.0
1-11	1218.1	1631	421	79.5 H	62.2
1-18	1227.4	1639	429	79.3	69.8
1-25	1276.1	1662	429	79.5 H	79.4 H
2-1	1277.7	1261	748	62.8	73.9
2-8	1290.0	1522	512	74.8	72.4
2-15	1282.0	1133	877	56.4	64.7
2-22	1275.8	776	1209	39.1	56.8
3-1	1299.4	1129	851	57.0	50.8
3-8	1269.7	687	1310	34.4	43.5
3-15	1247.4	759	1204	38.7	43.4
3-22	1267.5	1075	933	53.5	42.2
3-29	1266.8	1226	756	61.9	51.4
4-4	1259.0	845	1065	44.2	53.2
4-12	1265.7	1216	753	61.8	56.0
4-19	1266.6	1143	841	57.6	54.5
4-26	1275.2	1103	867	56.0	58.5
5-3	1247.2	700	1246	36.0	49.9
5-10	1274.2	1469	546	72.9	55.0
5-17	1285.3	1419	593	70.5	59.8
5-24	1302.0	1141	862	57.0	66.8
5-31	1315.4	1146	804	58.8	62.1
6-7	1316.4	1296	764	62.9	59.6
6-14	1301.0	872	1125	43.7	55.1
6-21	1324.5	1234	749	62.2	56.3
6-28	1335.5	1271	709	64.2	56.7
7-5	1334.5	1245	709	63.7	63.4
7-12	1338.6	1147	832	58.0	62.0
7-19	1359.5	1361	653	67.6	63.1
7-26	1357.1	729	1287	36.2	53.9
8-2	1353.0	882	1110	44.3	49.4
8-9	1320.8	616	1372	31.0	37.2
8-16	1312.7	802	1129	41.5	38.9

Table 6-2 (Cont'd)

Week Ending	DJIA	Weekly Advances	Weekly Declines	% Advanced	3-Week Mov.Av.
8-23	1318.3	1070	850	55.7	42.7
8-30	1334.0	1183	752	61.1	52.8
9-6	1335.7	758	1146	39.8	52.2
9-13	1307.7	459	1588	22.4 L	41.1
9-20	1297.9	865	1087	44.3	35.5 L
9-26	1320.8	766	1150	40.0	35.6
10-4	1328.7	1186	756	61.1	48.5
10-11	1339.9	1026	913	52.9	51.3
10-18	1368.8	1288	648	66.5	60.2
10-25	1356.5	1050	921	53.3	57.6
11-1	1390.3	1356	633	68.2	62.7
11-8	1404.4	1459	561	72.2	64.6
11-15	1435.1	1436	566	71.7	70.7
11-22	1464.3	1432	604	70.3	71.4
11-29	1472.1	1055	846	55.5	65.8
12-6	1477.2	1147	838	57.8	61.2
12-13	1535.2	1526	562	73.1	62.1
12-20	1543.0	1158	895	56.4	62.4
12-27	1543.0	885	1053	45.7	58.4
1-3-86	1549.2	1333	629	67.9	56.7
1-10	1513.5	767	1310	36.9	50.2
1-17	1536.7	1382	624	68.9	57.9
1-24	1529.9	908	1082	45.6	50.5
1-31	1571.0	1377	661	67.6	60.7
2-7	1613.4	1330	706	65.3	59.5
2-14	1664.5	1490	560	72.7	68.5
2-21	1697.7	1502	519	74.3	70.8
2-28	1709.1	1382	688	66.8	71.3
3-7	1699.8	1231	812	60.3	67.1
3-14	1792.7	1586	461	77.5 H	68.2
3-21	1768.6	1097	969	53.1	63.6
3-27	1821.7	1187	835	58.7	63.1
4-4	1739.2	667	1407	32.2	48.0
4-11	1790.2	1480	536	73.4	54.8
4-18	1840.4	1498	521	74.2	59.9
4-25	1835.6	949	1061	47.2	64.9
5-2	1774.7	516	1505	25.5	49.0
5-9	1789.4	1246	719	63.4	45.4
5-16	1759.8	717	1285	35.8	41.6 L
5-23	1823.3	1323	656	66.9	55.4
5-30	1876.7	1235	718	63.2	55.3
6-6	1885.9	773	1195	39.3	56.5
6-13	1874.2	877	1069	45.1	49.2

60

3. The pattern of the Diffusion Index was similar to the pattern of the DJIA in 1984, moving down gradually in the first half of the year and then recovered and stabilized in the second half of the year.

4. In the first half of 1985, the pattern of the Diffusion Index was similar to the movement of the DJIA. However, in the second half of the year the DJIA exhibited a stronger pattern than that of the Diffusion Index.

5. For the first half of 1986, the DJIA moved up strongly while the Diffusion Index was at first showing strength and then started to weaken. This could be the sign that the long awaited "correction" of the bull market may not be far away.

CONCLUSIONS

On the basis of both logic and empirical evidence we strongly feel that a study of the movements in both the DJIA and the Diffusion Index can improve one's judgement as to the probable future direction of the stock market.

The Diffusion Index, like the rate of change, can lead the aggregate. At times, the experienced investor can obtain clear messages from the Diffusion Index.

UPDATE—RECENT DEVELOPMENTS IN THE STOCK MARKET DURING THE PERIOD FROM JUNE 13, 1986 TO FEB. 13, 1987

To bring my readers up to date, I've prepared a supplement to Table 6-2 and a chart on the Diffusion Index of Advancing Issues on NYSE during the latest seven months from June 13, 1986 to Feb. 13, 1987. Examination of the data and the chart indicates the following:

1. There were three low points of the Diffusion Index during this period. They occurred on 7-25-86, 9-19-86, and 12-26-86. The recovery from these low points seemed to lead the advance of the DJIA by 1 to 2 weeks.

2. The decline from the high point which the Diffusion Index reached on Aug. 29, 1986 was one week earlier than the decline in the DJIA.

3. The strength of the Diffusion Index in Sept. and Oct. of 1986 had a parallel rise in the DJIA. However, the weakness in the Diffusion Index in the last few weeks of Dec. 1986 was accompanied only by sidewise fluctuation in the DJIA without a decline.

4. The substantial rise in the DJIA since the beginning of 1987 accompanied a substantial rise in the Diffusion Index.

(continued after Table and Chart Supplements)

Table 6-2 Supplement
DIFFUSION INDEX OF ADVANCING ISSUES ON NYSE

Week Ending	DJIA	Weekly Advances	Weekly Declines	% Advanced	3-wk. Mov.Av.
6-20-86	1879.5	817	1187	40.8	41.7
6-27	1885.3	1263	725	63.5	49.8
7-3	1900.9	1177	756	60.9	55.1
7-11	1821.4	546	1475	27.0	50.5
7-18	1778.0	679	1322	33.9	40.6
7-25	1810.0	1147	837	57.8	39.6
8-1	1763.6	586	1410	29.4	40.4
8-8	1782.6	1063	884	54.6	47.3
8-15	1855.6	1637	385	81.0	55.0
8-22	1887.8	1252	748	62.6	66.1
8-29	1898.3	1216	795	60.5	68.0
9-5	1899.8	958	995	49.1	57.4
9-12	1758.7	300	1814	14.2	41.3
9-19	1762.7	1047	937	52.8	38.7
9-26	1769.7	1185	781	60.3	42.4
10-3	1774.2	1100	858	56.2	56.4
10-10	1793.2	1123	800	58.4	58.3
10-17	1837.0	1189	721	62.3	59
10-23	1832.3	1046	937	52.7	57.8
10-31	1877.8	1394	589	70.3	61.8
11-7	1886.5	1210	755	61.6	61.5
11-14	1873.6	857	1089	44.0	58.6
11-21	1893.6	792	1167	40.4	48.7
11-28	1914.2	1088	820	57.0	47.1
12-7	1925.0	1114	828	57.4	51.6
12-14	1912.2	606	1367	30.7	48.4
12-20	1928.9	1065	929	53.4	47.2
12-26	1930.4	709	1226	36.6	40.2
1-2-87	1927.3	1047	875	54.4	48.1
1-9	2005.9	1885	228	89.2	60.1
1-16	2076.6	1440	596	70.7	71.4
1-23	2101.5	1118	867	56.3	72.1
1-30	2158.0	1181	768	60.6	62.5
2-6	2186.8	1552	477	76.5	64.5
2-13	2183.3	1023	956	51.7	62.9

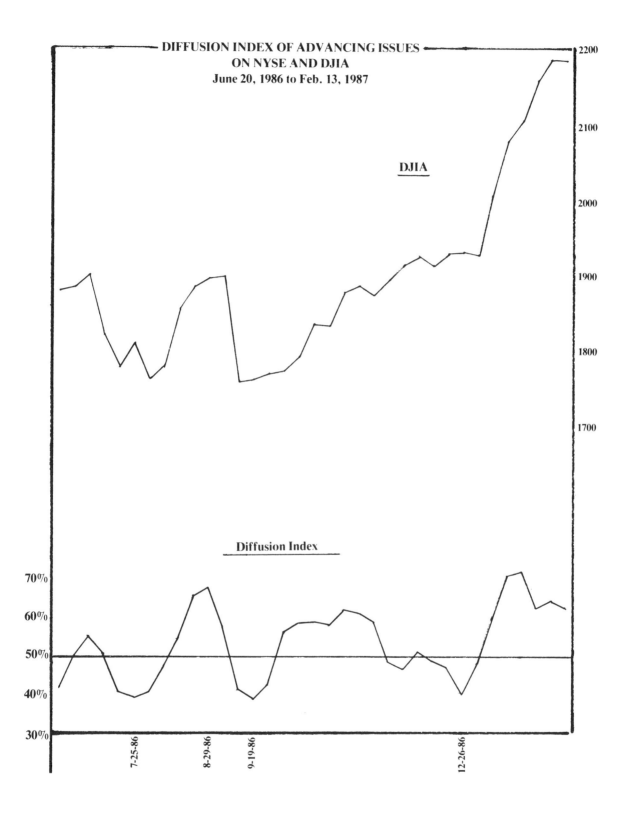

DIFFUSION INDEX OF ADVANCING ISSUES
ON NYSE AND DJIA
June 20, 1986 to Feb. 13, 1987

DJIA

Diffusion Index

63

5. The analysis of recent experience indicates that the Diffusion Index is useful in two ways. One is to indicate the strength of the current move in the DJIA. The other is to occasionally foretell the possibility of change in the direction of movement of stock prices, as measured by a market index like the DJIA.

Chapter 7

Volume Leads Price

The relationships between stock price and volume changes has been long considered of vital importance in predicting future movements of stock prices, both stock averages and individual issues. However, up until now there were very few serious studies undertaken to scientifically study their relationships. On the other hand, there was no lack of common beliefs in the marketplace about the relationships between stock prices and volume of sales.

Since the correct interpretation of the impact of volume changes on share prices represents one of the important keys to the prediction of future market movements, the commonly held beliefs should be carefully compared to findings which are derived from properly designed empirical and deductive analysis.

PRICE VS. VOLUME CHANGES

As mentioned above, students of technical market analysis consider the relationships between stock price and volume changes of vital importance in predicting future movement of stock prices, both of stock averages and individual issues. Generally, they believe that volume goes with trend of price. Specifically, they mean:

1. When volume tends to increase during price declines, it is a bearish indication.
2. When volume tends to increase during advances, it is a bullish indication.
3. When volume tends to decrease during price declines, it is bullish.

4. When volume tends to decrease during price advances, it is bearish.

Since the pattern of price-volume relationships constitutes one of the cornerstones of technical market analysis, more careful analysis of price-volume relationships seems very worthwhile. Two types of analysis are accordingly introduced below. First, the stock market pricing mechanism is examined in terms of basic principles of economics, observations, and deductive reasoning to see whether there is a pattern of changes in volume and stock price. Second, the pattern of changes in price and volume is examined on the basis of empirical evidence.

Supply and Demand in the Stock Market. The stock market is usually cited in basic economic texts as a classic example of pure competition where the price of a stock at any given moment is determined by "bids" and "asks" of buyers and sellers.

Changeability and Volatility of Demand for Stocks. The factors underlying demand for stocks are many. The more important factors are (1) previous stock price rise and expectation of the same in the near future, (2) fear of erosion of purchasing power of fixed income from more inflation, (3) expectation of increase of dividend and earnings from cyclical upturn or growth of the company, or from the secular growth of the economy, (4) expectation of better overall return (dividend and appreciation) over bonds and other financial media, and so forth.

From the above factors it can be seen that the demand for stocks is strongly influenced by the expectations of investors. Expectations, however, are highly psychological. They can be quickly changed not only by future developments of all sorts (social, economic, political, domestic, or international), but also by interpretations of those developments. Therefore, the demand for a specific stock or stocks in general is subject to frequent and swift changes, both upward or downward.

Supply of Stock is Less Changeable and Less Volatile. Relying on observations and common sense, we know that owners of stocks have a special attachment to the original purchase price. Theoretically, decision of sale should be made in terms of what one thinks one can gain from it in the future rather than what it cost in the past. However, the behavior of human beings is seldom dominated wholly by logical reasoning. Besides, even if we adhere to logic, who knows for sure what the future would bring us from it? On the other hand, it is hard to admit to oneself and others that the purchase was a failure and has to be written off at whatever salvage value. Because of the special attachment to the original purchase price and the influence of inertia, the sellers as a group, in our view, are more passively motivated than buyers. Consequently, the change of supply tends to be less frequent and of smaller magnitude compared to the change in demand.

Changes in Demand vs. Changes in Supply. The demand for, and supply of stocks at a given moment of time are influenced by more or less the same set of circumstances. If a favorable set of circumstances or factors is reflected in an increase of demand, the latter must be accompanied by less willingness to sell on the part of the owners. In other words, we should normally expect increases in demand to be associated with reduction in supply, and vice-versa. However, in view of the special characteristics of sellers as a group just discussed, an increase in demand is likely to be accompanied by a smaller change (reduction) in supply. By the same token, a reduction in demand should be associated with a smaller increase in supply. In other words, demand is a more dynamic force than supply in determining changes in stock prices.

Price and Volume Changes Under Changing Demand and Supply. Case A in Figure 7-1 shows changes in prices and volume under conditions of increasing demand with less than proportionate reduction in supply, and case B under conditions of decreasing demand with less than proportionate increase in supply. What we find in both cases is that price advances with volume increasing, and price declines with volume decreasing. In other words, changes in price and volume usually go together in the same direction. This partially contradicts the assumptions of technical market students on price-volume relationships. The suggestion that a volume decrease during price declines is bullish does not seem to correspond to what we deductively find from basic economic principles and observations of the behavior pattern of stock buyers and sellers.

Empirical Study on Market Prices and Volume of Sales. Careful empirical studies on relationships between changes in market prices and changes in volume of sales were conducted by C. Ying in his *"Market Prices and Volumes of Sales."* His findings are:

1. A small volume is usually accompanied by a fall in price.
2. A large volume is usually accompanied by a rise in price.
3. A large increase in volume is usually accompanied by either a large rise in price or a large fall in price.
4. A large volume is usually followed by a rise in price.
5. If the volume has been decreasing consecutively for a period of five trading days, there will be a tendency for the price to fall over the next four trading days.

Figure 7-1

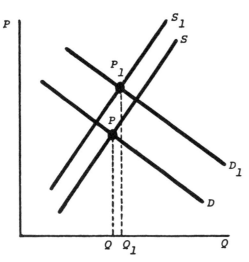

Case A. Increase in demand with less than proportionate reduction in supply.

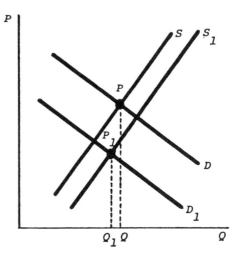

Case B. Decrease in demand with less than proportionate increase in supply.

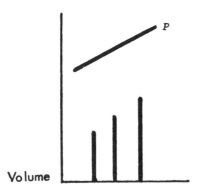

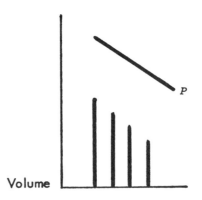

Conventional chart of price and volume as reported in daily newspapers.

68

6. If the volume has been increasing consecutively for a period of five trading days, there will be a tendency for the price to rise over the next four trading days.

The above empirical findings seem to correspond closely to what we find on the basis of deductive reasoning. A declining market should normally be accompanied by a small volume of transactions. The view of technical market students that a volume decrease during price declines is bullish may be seriously in error.

CORRECT INTERPRETATIONS

The gist of our discussions above on price vs. volume changes can be summarized in a few statements as follows:

1. Stock prices are determined by supply and demand.
2. The demand for stocks is more volatile and changeable than the supply of stocks.
3. Changes in stock prices are caused more by shifts in demand than by shifts in supply.
4. Changes in prices and volume usually go in the same direction. In other words, price advance is usually accompanied by increasing volume and price decline by decreasing volume.
5. A small volume is usually accompanied by a fall in price. A large volume is usually accompanied by a rise in price.

PRICE AND VOLUME CHANGES OVER A MARKET CYCLE

What we have discussed so far are the general relationships between price and volume changes and their underlying factors of supply and demand. Now, we want to go a step further to introduce the characteristic patterns between volume and price changes during four different phases (up, top, decline, and bottom) over a market cycle in stock prices.

Based on the general principles just discussed on price and volume changes, and also our observations of the stock market over many years in the past, we can discern the characteristic patterns during four different phases of a stock market cycle as follows:

69

Four Phases Of A Market Cycle

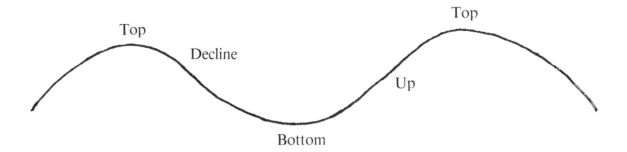

The Up Phase of a Market Cycle

1. When the broad market index of stock prices is increasing, the total volume transacted on the NYSE is also increasing.
2. The trend of daily volume has been rising.
3. When stock prices decline, volume is also decreasing.

The Top Phase of a Market Cycle

1. The broad market index of stock prices is sidewise, but the market volume is rising.
2. The trend of daily volume is neutral, but the total volume has been high.
3. When stock prices decline, volume declines also.

The Down Phase of a Market Cycle

1. When stock prices decline, volume is also declining.
2. The trend of daily volume has been declining.
3. When stock prices move up, volume is moderate.

The Bottom Phase of a Market Cycle

1. Stock prices are sidewise, volume is low.
2. When stock prices advance, volume remains low.
3. When stock prices decline, volume is low.

REVIEW OF RECORD
OF VOLUME DURING THE PERIOD
FROM JAN. 1982 TO JUNE 1986 ON NYSE

Table 7-1 shows the following statistics for the period from Jan. 1982 to June 1986:

1. Average daily volume each week on NYSE.
2. 3-week and 10-week moving averages of average daily volume on NYSE.
3. Ratio between average daily up volume and down volume on NYSE.
4. 3-week and 10-week moving averages of the ratio between average daily up volume and average daily down volume.
5. Dow-Jones Industrial Average. These statistics are also charted in Figure 7-2.

Level of Volume

Examinations of the record during the 4½ years from 1982 through 1986 in Figure 7-2 and Table 7-1 enable us to formulate some rough ideas as to what constitutes high, medium, or low volume of transactions on the NYSE and what the implications are on future price movements.

As shown in the accompanying table below, an average daily volume in the area of 70 - 90 million shares on NYSE is considered low volume. Low volume is most often associated with falling price. On the other hand, when volume reached 110 million shares or above, the stock market was most often found in rising prices. A volume in the area between 90 and 110 million shares was found associated with rising prices as often as with falling prices. The implication of medium volume was not clear. A better indication will be found, however, when volume momentum or trend is evaluated.

Average Daily Volume on NYSE	Classification	Accompanied Usually by	Outlook
70-90 mil. shares	Low volume	Falling prices	Bearish
90-110 mil. shares	Medium volume	Sidewise prices	Indeterminate
Over 110 mil. shares	High volume	Rising prices	Bullish

Table 7-1
3-WEEK & 10-WEEK MOVING AVERAGES OF AVERAGE DAILY VOLUME
AND THE RATIO BETWEEN UP VOLUME & DOWN VOLUME ON NYSE
Jan. 1982 to Sept. 1984

Date	DJIA	Av.Daily Vol. (in Thousands) NYSE	3-Wk. Mov.Av.	10-Wk. Mov.Av.	Av.Daily Up Vol. NYSE	Down Vol. NYSE	Up Vol./ Down Vol.	3-Wk. Mov.Av.	10-Wk. Mov.Av.
1-8-82	866.5	44248	–	–	15.49	23.58	0.66	–	–
1-15	847.6	47420	–	–	15.55	26.94	0.58	–	–
1-22	845	46371	46.01	–	18.26	22.29	0.82	0.69	–
1-29	871.1	63463	52.42	–	33.21	16.41	2.02	1.14	–
2-5	851	49793	53.21	–	20.44	23.95	0.85	1.23	–
2-12	833.8	46649	53.30	–	15.31	26.32	0.58	1.15	–
2-19	824.3	52173	49.54	–	21.55	23.65	0.91	0.78	–
2-26	824.4	56263	51.70	–	25.81	16.17	1.60	1.03	–
3-5	807.4	65774	58.07	–	23.24	35.36	0.66	1.06	–
3-12	797.4	61079	61.04	53.32	25.46	28.67	0.89	1.05	0.96
3-19	805.7	48605	58.49	53.76	25.68	16.32	1.57	1.04	1.05
3-26	817.9	53697	54.46	54.39	29.44	18.84	1.56	1.34	1.15
4-2	838.6	48284	50.20	54.58	27.82	13.73	2.03	1.72	1.27
4-8	842.9	50859	50.95	53.32	26.43	16.38	1.61	1.73	1.23
4-16	843.2	48386	49.17	53.18	23.66	16.42	1.44	1.69	1.29
4-23	862.2	61443	53.56	54.66	33.23	20.30	1.64	1.56	1.39
4-30	848.4	53377	54.40	54.78	20.16	26.27	0.77	1.28	1.38
5-7	869.2	59760	58.19	55.13	35.75	16.47	2.17	1.53	1.43
5-14	857.8	53666	55.60	53.92	22.43	23.92	0.94	1.29	1.46
5-21	835.9	47404	53.61	52.55	13.83	26.87	0.51	1.21	1.42
5-28	819.5	44483	48.52	52.14	10.68	26.94	0.40	0.62	1.31
6-4	805	45860	45.92	51.35	16.44	24.41	0.67	0.53	1.22
6-11	809.7	53359	47.90	51.86	25.46	20.72	1.23	0.77	1.14
6-18	788.6	48861	49.37	51.66	12.21	29.46	0.41	0.77	1.02
6-25	803.1	52593	51.61	52.08	27.23	19.26	1.41	1.02	1.02
7-2	797	48930	50.13	50.83	19.13	22.97	0.83	0.88	0.93
7-9	814.1	55102	52.21	51.00	30.81	20.99	1.47	1.24	1.00
7-16	828.7	63752	55.93	51.40	32.27	23.37	1.38	1.23	0.93
7-23	830.6	56403	58.42	51.68	26.26	22.02	1.19	1.35	0.95
7-30	808.6	46454	55.54	51.58	11.84	28.90	0.41	0.99	0.94
8-6	784.3	54152	52.34	52.55	17.11	31.20	0.55	0.72	0.96
8-13	788.1	50205	50.27	52.98	19.73	23.44	0.84	0.60	0.97
8-20	869.3	105651	70.00	58.21	64.13	19.81	3.24	1.54	1.17
8-27	883.5	109966	88.61	64.32	66.81	34.04	1.96	2.01	1.33
9-3	925.1	86881	100.83	67.75	55.51	24.12	2.30	2.50H	1.42
9-10	906.8	72769	89.87	70.13	29.55	34.90	0.85	1.70	1.42
9-17	916.9	71021	76.89	71.73	36.57	26.73	1.37	1.51	1.41
9-24	919.5	75468	73.09	72.90	34.88	31.76	1.10	1.11	1.38
10-1	907.7	60182	68.89	73.27	24.64	28.12	0.88	1.12	1.35
10-8	986.9	97669	77.77	78.40	71.27	19.85	3.59H	1.86	1.67
10-15	993.1	118489H	92.11	84.83	69.20	41.58	1.66	2.04	1.78
10-22	1031.5	101386	105.85H	89.95	70.36	33.19	2.12	2.46	1.91H
10-29	991.7	83168	101.02	87.70	32.70	43.01	0.76	1.51	1.66

Table 7-1 (Cont'd)

Date	DJIA	Av.Daily Vol. (in Thousands) NYSE	3-Wk. Mov.Av.	10-Wk. Mov.Av.	Av.Daily Up Vol. NYSE	Down Vol. NYSE	Up Vol./ Down Vol.	3-Wk. Mov.Av.	10-Wk. Mov.Av.
11-5	1051.8	112251	98.94	87.93	74.85	27.92	2.68	1.85	1.73
11-12	1039.9	94638	96.69	88.71	42.13	43.86	0.96	1.47	1.60
11-19	1021.3	82838	96.58	89.71	31.74	42.76	0.74	1.46	1.59
11-26	1007.4	63465	80.31	88.96	23.77	33.03	0.72	0.81	1.52
12-3	1031.4	82315	76.21	89.64	42.02	31.54	1.33	0.93	1.54
12-10	1018.8	93941	79.91	93.02H	45.77	39.67	1.15	1.07	1.57
12-17	1011.5	78457	84.90	91.10	29.60	41.02	0.72	1.07	1.28
12-23	1045.1	71646	81.35	86.41	30.24	24.48	1.60	1.16	1.28
12-31	1046.5	55319	68.47	81.81	28.14	20.59	1.37	1.23	1.20
1-7-83	1076.1	97348	74.77	83.22	59.70	30.67	1.95	1.64	1.32
1-14	1080.9	94702	82.46	81.47	51.99	33.27	1.56	1.63	1.21
1-21	1053.0	81688	91.25	80.17	32.48	40.80	0.80	1.44	1.19
1-28	1064.8	84379	86.92	80.33	41.03	36.81	1.11	1.16	1.23
2-4	1077.9	78602	81.56	81.84	40.57	29.32	1.38	1.10	1.30
2-11	1086.5	85471	82.82	82.16	43.99	32.21	1.37	1.29	1.30
2-18	1092.8	79228	81.10	80.68	36.24	33.12	1.09	1.28	1.30
2-25	1120.9	95598	86.77	82.40	53.51	31.65	1.69	1.38	1.39
3-4	1141.0	101099	91.98	85.34	61.98	29.25	2.12	1.63	1.44
3-11	1117.7	82070	92.92	88.02	32.59	38.98	0.84	1.55	1.39
3-18	1117.7	70644	84.60	85.35	27.62	34.10	0.81	1.26	1.28
3-25	1140.1	83283	78.67	84.21	45.11	29.88	1.51	1.05	1.27
3-31	1130.0	75050	76.33	83.54	34.01	31.49	1.08	1.13	1.30
4-8	1124.7	71429	76.59	82.25	29.79	32.58	0.91	1.17	1.28
4-15	1171.3	88325	78.27	83.22	56.47	21.70	2.60H	1.53	1.40
4-22	1196.3	97606	85.79	84.43	53.24	35.18	1.51	1.67	1.42
4-29	1226.2	101146	95.69	86.63	54.80	35.60	1.54	1.88H	1.46
5-6	1232.6	103097H	100.62H	87.37	59.84	34.21	1.75	1.60	1.47H
5-13	1218.8	92943	99.06	86.56	43.57	39.16	1.11	1.47	1.37
5-20	1190.0	82412	92.82	86.59	33.93	39.16	0.87	1.24	1.37
5-27	1216.1	97432	90.93	89.27	50.93	35.39	1.44	1.14	1.43
6-3	1213.0	82809	87.55	89.22	38.49	35.36	1.09	1.13	1.39
6-10	1196.1	87749	89.33	90.49	39.23	39.86	0.98	1.17	1.38
6-17	1242.2	99989	90.18	93.35	56.72	33.02	1.72	1.26	1.46
6-24	1241.7	93606	93.78	93.88H	47.36	35.16	1.35	1.35	1.34
7-1	1225.3	75019	89.54	91.62	32.21	34.83	0.92	1.33	1.28
7-8	1207.2	79200	82.60	89.20	30.60	40.60	0.75	1.01	1.20
7-15	1192.3	69500	74.60	85.80	26.70	35.00	0.76	0.81	1.10
7-22	1231.0	84600	77.80	85.00	16.70	30.30	1.54	1.02	1.14
7-29	1199.2	80000	87.60	84.70	28.60	52.20	0.55	0.95	1.11
8-5	1183.0	80200	81.60	83.00	30.00	41.40	0.72	0.94	1.04
8-12	1182.8	75600	78.60	82.50	37.60	31.10	1.21	0.83	1.05
8-19	1194.2	76800	77.50	81.50	39.50	29.20	1.35	1.09	1.09
8-26	1192.1	69400	73.90	78.40	27.40	33.70	0.81	1.12	1.00
9-2	1215.4	66300	70.80	75.70	37.00	22.20	1.67	1.28	1.03
9-9	1239.7	84700	73.50	76.60	46.40	30.60	1.52	1.33	1.09
9-16	1225.7	81400	77.50	76.90	35.90	36.90	0.97	1.39	1.11
9-23	1255.5	94000	86.70	79.30	52.70	31.40	1.68	1.39	1.20
9-30	1233.1	77600	84.30	78.60	27.80	40.80	0.68	1.11	1.12

73

Table 7-1 (Cont'd)

Date	DJIA	Av.Daily Vol. (in Thousands) NYSE	3-Wk. Mov.Av.	10-Wk. Mov.Av.	Av.Daily Up Vol. NYSE	Down Vol. NYSE	Up Vol./ Down Vol.	3-Wk. Mov.Av.	10-Wk. Mov.Av.
10-7	1272.1	98200	89.90	80.40	58.6	30.4	1.93	1.43	1.25
10-14	1263.5	72300	82.70	79.60	27.2	37.7	0.72	1.11	1.25
10-21	1248.8	90900	87.10	81.20	32.0	51.0	0.63	1.09	1.20
10-28	1223.5	81600	81.60	81.60	31.6	40.3	0.78	0.71	1.14
11-3	1218.3	83200	85.20	83.00	38.3	35.4	1.08	0.83	1.17
11-10	1250.2	76100	80.30	84.00	41.8	26.6	1.57	1.14	1.16
11-17	1251.1	83400	80.90	83.90	38.6	34.9	1.11	1.25	1.12
11-24	1277.4	95300	84.90	85.30	52.8	32.4	1.63	1.44	1.18
12-2	1265.2	99900	92.90	85.90	42.9	43.6	0.98	1.24	1.11
12-9	1260.1	95700	97.00	87.70	38.9	44.8	0.86	1.16	1.13
12-17	1242.1	85100	93.60	86.40	31.3	42.6	0.73	0.86	1.01
12-24	1250.5	87200	89.30	87.80	38.6	36.6	1.05	0.88	1.04
12-30	1258.6	77000	83.10	86.50	37.2	28.7	1.30	1.03	1.11
1-7-84	1286.6	120000	94.70	90.30	80.3	30.1	2.67	1.67	1.30
1-14	1270.1	103300	100.10	92.30	43.1	48.4	0.89	1.62	1.28
1-21	1259.1	97500	106.90	94.40	40.0	46.9	0.85	1.47	1.21
1-27	1230.0	102700	101.20	96.40	40.1	51.6	0.78	0.84	1.17
2-3	1197.1	108900	103.00	97.70	40.1	58.2	0.69	0.77	1.08
2-10	1160.7	106800	105.80	98.40	35.1	62.6	0.56	0.68	1.04
2-17	1148.9	84700	100.10	97.30	33.1	41.8	0.79	0.68	1.03
2-24	1165.1	91200	94.20	97.90	42.0	39.3	1.07	0.81	1.07
3-2	1171.1	94700	90.20	98.70	53.9	32.4	1.66	1.17	1.13
3-9	1139.8	79500	88.50	98.90	24.2	46.0	0.53	1.09	1.05
3-16	1184.3	92300	88.80	96.20	58.8	23.8	2.47	1.55	1.03
3-23	1154.8	81000	84.30	93.90	32.5	39.7	0.82	1.27	1.02
3-30	1164.9	80100	84.50	92.20	55.9	28.3	1.98	1.76	1.14
4-6	1132.2	91000	84.00	91.00	33.8	51.7	0.65	1.15	1.12
4-13	1150.1	85400	85.50	88.70	42.8	33.1	1.29	1.31	1.18
4-20	1158.1	83200	86.50	86.30	37.8	28.9	1.31	1.08	1.26
4-27	1169.1	86000	84.90	86.40	45.7	31.0	1.47	1.36	1.33
5-4	1165.3	96200	88.50	86.90	46.6	37.8	1.23	1.34	1.34
5-11	1157.1	87900	90.00	86.30	35.6	41.9	0.85	1.18	1.26
5-18	1133.8	82800	89.00	86.60	28.0	44.6	0.63	0.90	1.27
5-25	1107.1	84200	85.00	85.80	23.6	49.8	0.47	0.65	1.07
6-1	1124.4	88200	85.10	86.50	45.3	34.0	1.33	0.81	1.12
6-8	1131.3	83000	85.10	86.80	42.6	28.5	1.49	1.10	1.07
6-15	1086.9	77200	82.80	85.40	19.5	48.3	0.40	1.07	1.05
6-22	1131.1	101000	87.10	87.00	61.3	28.2	2.17	1.35	1.14
6-29	1132.4	80500	86.20	86.70	34.5	30.6	1.13	1.23	1.12
7-6	1122.6	67800	83.10	84.90	25.8	31.5	0.82	1.37	1.05
7-13	1109.9	80000	76.10	83.30	28.9	39.9	0.72	0.89	1.00
7-20	1101.4	79400	75.70	82.40	29.8	39.6	0.75	0.76	0.99
7-27	1114.6	86900	82.10	82.80	43.1	35.6	1.21	0.89	1.05
8-3	1202.1	140000	102.10	88.40	108.1	24.0	4.50H	2.15	1.45
8-10	1218.1	150900H	125.90H	94.70	85.4	55.0	1.55	2.42H	1.47
8-17	1211.9	83200	124.70	94.70	35.8	38.1	0.94	2.33	1.42
8-25	1236.5	94500	109.50	96.40	54.1	29.9	1.81	1.43	1.56
8-31	1224.4	69400	82.40	93.30	32.0	28.3	1.13	1.61	1.46
9-7	1207.4	76800	80.20	92.90	31.7	35.8	0.89	1.28	1.43

74

Table 7-1 (Cont'd)

Date	DJIA	Av.Daily Vol. (in Thousands) NYSE	3-Wk. Mov.Av.	10-Wk. Mov.Av.	Av.Daily UP Vol. NYSE	Down Vol. NYSE	Up Vol./ Down Vol.	3-Wk. Mov.Av.	10-Wk. Mov.Av.
9-14	1237.5	100300	82.2	96.1	60.3	28.8	2.09	1.37	1.56
9-21	1201.7	105800	94.3	98.7	42.4	50.9	0.83	1.27	1.57
9-28	1206.7	86100	97.4	99.4 H	39.3	35.0	1.12	1.35	1.61H
10-5	1182.5	83000	91.6	99.0	26.9	44.5	0.60	0.85	1.55
10-12	1190.7	79000	82.7	92.9	39.0	27.1	1.44	1.05	1.24
10-19	1225.9	121400	94.5	90.0	67.4	42.7	1.58	1.21	1.24
10-26	1205.0	88200	96.2	90.5	30.6	45.8	0.67	1.23	1.22
11-2	1216.7	90900	100.2	90.1	50.9	29.1	1.75	1.33	1.21
11-9	1219.0	93800	91.0	92.5	46.5	35.6	1.31	1.24	1.23
11-16	1187.9	72800	85.8	92.1	18.9	42.5	0.44	1.17	1.18
11-23	1220.3	77100	81.2	89.8	42.1	24.6	1.71	1.15	1.15
11-30	1188.9	82300	77.4	87.5	28.0	41.8	0.67	0.94	1.13
12-7	1163.2	88400	82.6	87.7	34.6	40.6	0.85	1.08	1.10
12-14	1175.9	83200	84.6	87.7	39.2	32.2	1.22	0.91	1.16
12-21	1199.0	118600	96.7	91.7	63.6	43.3	1.47	1.18	1.17
12-28	1204.2	62400	88.1	85.8	28.7	23.4	1.23	1.31	1.13
1-4-85	1185.0	78600	86.5	84.8	27.6	40.3	0.68	1.13	1.13
1-11	1218.1	102000	81.0	85.9	60.6	30.2	2.00	1.30	1.16
1-18	1227.4	126800	102.5	89.2	70.7	41.1	1.72	1.47	1.20
1-25	1276.1	149900	126.2	96.9	94.7	40.8	2.32	2.01H	1.39
2-1	1277.7	130400	135.7	102.3	63.2	50.7	1.25	1.76	1.34
2-8	1290.0	133300	137.9	107.4	81.4	39.3	2.07	1.88	1.48
2-15	1282.0	120800	128.2	110.6	56.6	51.3	1.10	1.47	1.51
2-22	1275.8	101600	118.6	112.4	37.0	50.4	0.73	1.30	1.46
3-1	1299.4	110400	110.9	111.6	60.5	36.8	1.64	1.16	1.47
3-8	1269.7	108800	106.9	116.3	36.3	57.8	0.63	1.00	1.41
3-15	1247.4	97500	105.6	118.2	36.0	46.6	0.77	1.01	1.42
3-22	1267.5	103200	103.2	118.3	52.8	38.1	1.39	0.93	1.36
3-29	1266.8	93400	98.0	114.9	51.0	31.8	1.35	1.17	1.33
4-4	1259.0	93500	96.7	109.3	36.8	43.6	0.84	1.19	1.18
4-12	1265.7	93300	93.4	105.6	49.6	32.1	1.55	1.25	1.21
4-19	1266.6	91400	92.4	101.4	41.5	37.3	1.11	1.17	1.11
4-26	1275.2	96700	93.8	99.0	45.0	39.3	1.15	1.27	1.12
5-3	1247.2	100900	96.3	98.9	40.6	49.0	0.83	1.03	1.13
5-10	1274.2	107700	101.8	98.6	68.2	27.7	2.46H	1.48	1.21
5-17	1285.3	102700	103.8	98.0	58.1	30.8	1.89	1.73	1.33
5-24	1302.0	113000	107.8	99.6	56.6	44.8	1.26	1.87	1.38
5-31	1315.4	107400	107.7	100.0	56.1	36.6	1.53	1.56	1.40
6-7	1316.4	120200	113.5	102.7	58.8	46.0	1.28	1.36	1.39
6-14	1301.0	97500	108.4	103.1	34.7	48.5	0.72	1.18	1.38
6-21	1324.5	102100	106.6	104.0	51.4	37.9	1.36	1.12	1.36
6-28	1335.5	89400	96.3	103.8	57.3	32.8	1.75	1.28	1.42
7-5	1334.5	92000	94.5	103.3	45.7	33.1	1.38	1.50	1.45
7-12	1338.6	106800	96.1	103.9	54.5	40.1	1.36	1.50	1.50
7-19	1359.5	128500	109.1	106.0	69.5	44.4	1.57	1.44	1.41
7=26	1357.1	119200	118.2	107.6	47.0	57.8	0.81	1.25	1.30

75

Table 7-1 (Cont'd)

Date	DJIA	Av.Daily Vol. (in Thousands) NYSE	3-Wk. Mov.Av.	10-Wk. Mov.Av.	Av.Daily Up Vol. NYSE	Down Vol. NYSE	Up Vol./ Down Vol.	3-Wk. Mov.Av.	10-Wk. Mov.Av.
8-2	1353.0	106400	118.0	107.0	50.9	44.7	1.14	1.17	1.29
8-9	1320.8	93900	106.5	105.6	37.0	45.6	0.81	0.92	1.22
8-16	1312.7	83500	94.6	101.9	30.6	40.0	0.77	0.91	1.17
8-23	1318.3	84000	87.1	100.6	41.7	30.6	1.36	0.98	1.23
8-30	1334.0	81700	83.1	98.5	40.1	29.6	1.35	1.16	1.23
9-6	1335.7	89100	84.9	98.5	33.9	40.3	0.84	1.18	1.14
9-13	1307.7	102700	91.2	99.6	29.6	60.2	0.49	0.89	1.05
9-20	1297.9	97200	96.3	98.6	39.7	44.8	0.89	0.74	1.00
9-26	1320.8	100200	100.0	95.8	43.6	45.3	0.96	0.78	0.94
10-4	1328.7	122000	106.5	96.1	60.4	47.7	1.27	1.04	0.99
10-11	1339.9	95800	106.0	95.0	47.0	36.3	1.29	1.17	1.00
10-18	1368.8	110800	109.5	96.7	60.5	37.7	1.60	1.39	1.08
10-25	1356.5	110700	105.8	99.4	53.4	44.8	1.19	1.36	1.12
11-1	1390.3	115900	112.5	102.6	63.1	38.9	1.62	1.47	1.15
11-8	1404.4	117500	114.7	106.2	64.2	38.0	1.69	1.50	1.18
11-15	1435.1	132400	121.9	110.5	76.5	41.9	1.83	1.71	1.28
11-22	1464.3	124800	124.9	112.7	70.8	38.8	1.82	1.78	1.42
11-29	1372.1	110600	122.6	114.1	53.7	43.5	1.23	1.63	1.45
12-6	1477.2	134600	123.3	117.5	62.5	56.2	1.11	1.39	1.47
12-13	1535.2	165500H	136.9	121.9	103.7	46.2	2.24	1.53	1.56H
12-20	1543.0	153400	151.2H	127.6H	73.1	64.3	1.14	1.50	1.55
12-27	1543.0	82500	133.8	124.8	32.9	38.4	0.86	1.41	1.47
1-3-86	1549.2	102200	112.7	123.9	51.7	35.4	1.46	1.15	1.50
1-10	1513.5	146400	110.4	127.0	58.6	75.5	0.78	1.03	1.42
1-17	1536.7	121500	123.4	127.4	63.0	45.0	1.40	1.21	1.39
1-24	1529.9	120800	129.6	126.2	48.3	56.9	0.85	1.01	1.29
1-31	1571.0	146200	129.5	128.4	81.0	51.4	1.58	1.28	1.27
2-7	1613.4	149200	138.7	132.2	76.0	51.4	1.48	1.30	1.29
2-14	1664.5	139900	145.1	132.8	82.1	42.4	1.94	1.67	1.37
2-21	1697.7	157400	148.8	132.0	94.5	49.1	1.92	1.78	1.34
2-28	1709.1	164800H	154.0	133.1	90.9	56.2	1.62	1.83H	1.39
3-7	1699.8	158800	160.3	140.7	74.6	68.1	1.10	1.55	1.41
3-14	1792.7	176200	166.6H	148.1	112.9	48.2	23.4H	1.67	1.50
3-21	1768.6	156600	163.9	149.1	68.7	70.3	0.98	1.47	1.52
3-27	1821.7	155700	162.8	152.6	91.5	50.5	1.81	1.71	1.56
4-4	1739.2	148500	153.6	155.3	44.4	88.5	0.50	1.10	1.53
4-11	1790.2	151300	151.8	155.8	87.5	46.2	1.89	1.40	1.56
4-18	1840.4	143900	147.9	155.3	81.5	47.4	1.72	1.37	1.58H
4-25	1835.6	147200	147.5	156.0H	63.6	68.8	0.92	1.51	1.48
5-2	1774.7	138500	143.2	154.2	45.3	79.8	0.57	1.07	1.35
5-9	1789.4	125400	137.0	150.2	65.5	45.2	1.45	0.98	1.33
5-16	1759.8	124300	129.4	146.8	43.5	64.7	0.67	0.90	1.29
5-23	1823.3	118200	122.6	141.0	71.8	32.4	2.22	1.45	1.27
5-30	1876.7	141900	128.1	139.5	82.9	45.0	1.84	1.58	1.36
6-6	1885.9	114800	125.0	135.4	45.9	52.6	0.87	1.64	1.27
6-13	1874.2	125200	127.3	133.1	58.6	52.6	1.11	1.27	1.33

H: High for the year

76

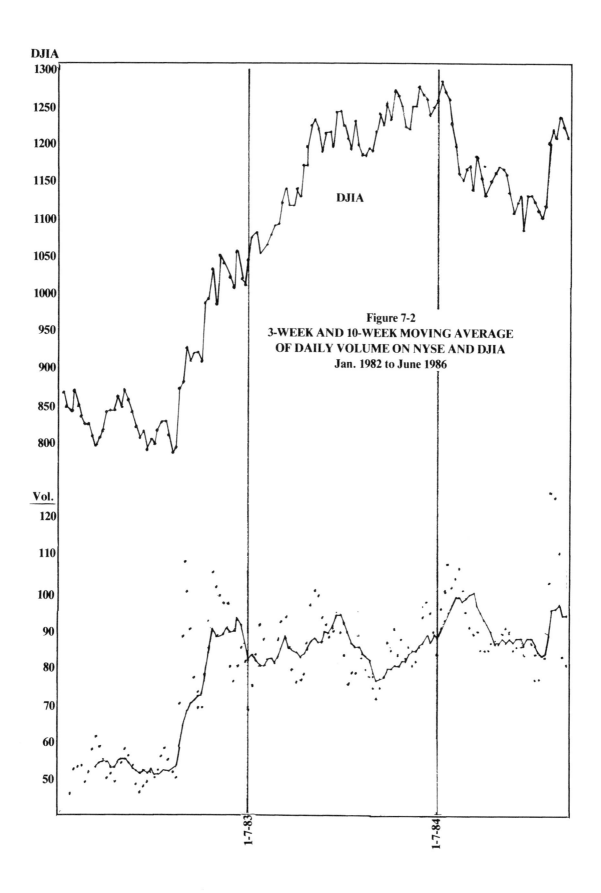

DJIA

1300
1250
1200
1150
1100
1050
1000
950
900
850
800

DJIA

Figure 7-2
3-WEEK AND 10-WEEK MOVING AVERAGE
OF DAILY VOLUME ON NYSE AND DJIA
Jan. 1982 to June 1986

Vol.

120
110
100
90
80
70
60
50

1-7-83

1-7-84

77

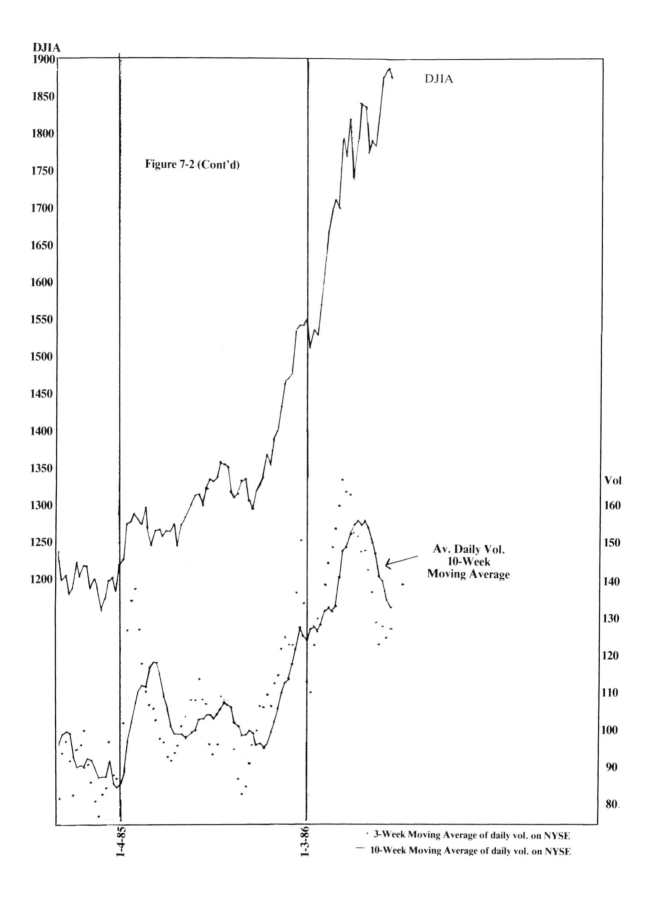

DJIA

Figure 7-2 (Cont'd)

DJIA

Av. Daily Vol.
10-Week
Moving Average

Vol.

1-4-85

1-3-86

· 3-Week Moving Average of daily vol. on NYSE
— 10-Week Moving Average of daily vol. on NYSE

UPDATE—RECENT DEVELOPMENTS IN THE STOCK MARKET DURING THE PERIOD FROM JUNE 13, 1986 to FEB. 13, 1987

To bring our readers up to date, I've prepared a supplement to Table 7-1 and a chart on the level of daily volume on NYSE. Examination of the data and the chart indicates the following:

1. The range of daily volume on NYSE (3-week moving average) during the latest seven months was between 122 million and 204 million shares. The mean volume was 163 million shares.

2. The range of daily volume in the first six months of 1986 was between 110 and 166 million shares. The mean volume was 138 million shares.

3. The level of volume in the last seven months was about 20% higher than the level in the first six months of 1986.

4. If we were to use the experience of the last 14 months *only* (Jan. 1986 to Feb. 1987) as a basis to classify the level of volume on NYSE into high, medium, and low categories, a rough guideline would be set as follows:

Average Daily Volume	Classification
Below 130 million	Low volume
130 million to 150 million	Medium volume
Over 150 million	High volume

5. The sharp increase in volume since the second week in Jan. 1987 was accompanied by a rise in DJIA of about 260 points over a period of six weeks. In the chart, we can see that the percentage rise in volume was greater than the rise of the DJIA. Volume was the driving force in the bull market.

Table 7-1 Supplement
3-WEEK & 10-WEEK MOVING AVERAGES OF AVERAGE DAILY VOLUME
AND THE RATIO BETWEEN UP VOLUME & DOWN VOLUME ON NYSE
Jan. 1982 to Sept. 1984

Date	DJIA	Av.Daily Vol. (in Thousands) NYSE	3-Wk. Mov.Av.	10-Wk. Mov.Av.	Av.Daily Up Vol. NYSE	Down Vol. NYSE	Up Vol./ Down Vol.	3-Wk. Mov.Av.	10-Wk. Mov.Av.
6-20-86	1879.5	125,956	122.0	130.5	55.0	56.3	0.98	0.99	1.24
6-27	1885.3	136,813	130.0	129.8	73.6	45.6	1.61	1.23	1.22
7-3	1900.9	135,250	132.7	128.6	72.1	47.2	1.53	1.37	1.29
7-11	1821.4	145,152	139.1	129.3	52.2	81.8	0.64	1.26	1.29
7-18	1778.0	150,043	143.5	131.8	52.4	84.1	0.62	0.93	1.21
7-25	1810.0	128,946	141.4	132.2	67.7	48.4	1.40	0.89	1.28
8-1	1763.6	123,587	134.2	132.8	40.8	67.1	0.61	0.88	1.12
8-8	1782.6	127,856	126.8	131.4	64.7	48.8	1.33	1.11	1.07
8-15	1855.6	132,209	127.9	133.1	92.6	28.2	3.28	1.74	1.31
8-22	1887.8	126,426	128.8	133.2	68.8	43.9	1.57	2.06	1.36
8-29	1898.3	130,923	129.9	133.7	68.7	48.6	1.41	2.09	1.40
9-5	1899.8	164,974	140.8	136.5	78.6	72.2	1.09	1.36	1.35
9-12	1758.7	182,042	159.3	141.2	38.2	130.2	0.29	0.93	1.22
9-19	1769.7	142,810	163.3	141	71.3	52.4	1.23	0.89	1.29
9-26	1774.2	128,560	151.1	138.8	64.0	52.4	1.30	0.94	1.35
10-3	1793.2	128,036	133.1	138.7	64.8	49.1	1.48	1.27	1.34
10-10	1837.0	122,707	126.4	138.6	62.9	43.6	1.48	1.34	1.43
10-17	1832.3	119,429	123.4	137.8	60.2	42.6	1.24	1.42	1.44
10-23	1877.8	124,286	122.1	137	97.3	48.6	2.14	1.40	1.24
10-31	1886.5	156,953	133.6	140	81.5	45.5	1.41	1.62	1.30
11-7	1873.6	158,443	146.6	142.8	66.0	57.8	1.06	1.60	1.30
11-14	1893.6	147,402	154.3	141	74.2	62.4	0.93	1.54	1.29
11-21	1914.2	172,119	159.3	140	70.8	80.1	1.45	1.13	1.36
11-28	1925.0	137,732	152.4	139.5	86.5	48.9	1.29	1.15	1.37
12-7	1912.2	172,216	160.7	143.9	46.4	67.0	0.61	1.22	1.38
12-14	1928.9	137,994	149.3	144.9	81.9	75.5	1.20	1.12	1.31
12-20	1930.4	170,764	160.3	149.7	42.9	68.5	0.70	1.03	1.28
12-26	1927.3	142,747	143.8	150	44.5	61	0.87	0.84	1.20
1-2-87	2005.9	114,262	135.9	149	136.0	51.2	3.76H	0.92	1.17
1-9	2076.0	189,914	142.3	152.3	124.7	36.2	1.86	1.78	1.33
1-16	2101.5	208,146	170.8	157.3	101.7	66.9	1.10	2.16	1.37
1-23	2158	212,604H	203.5H	163.8	94.2	92.3	1.39	2.24H	1.38
1-30	2186.8	179,115	199.9	164.5	126.9	67.6	2.11	1.45	1.42
2-6	2183.3	207,711	199.8	171.5	77.4	60.1	1.01	1.53	1.49H
2-13		173,938	186.9	171.7H		76.8		1.50	1.46

80

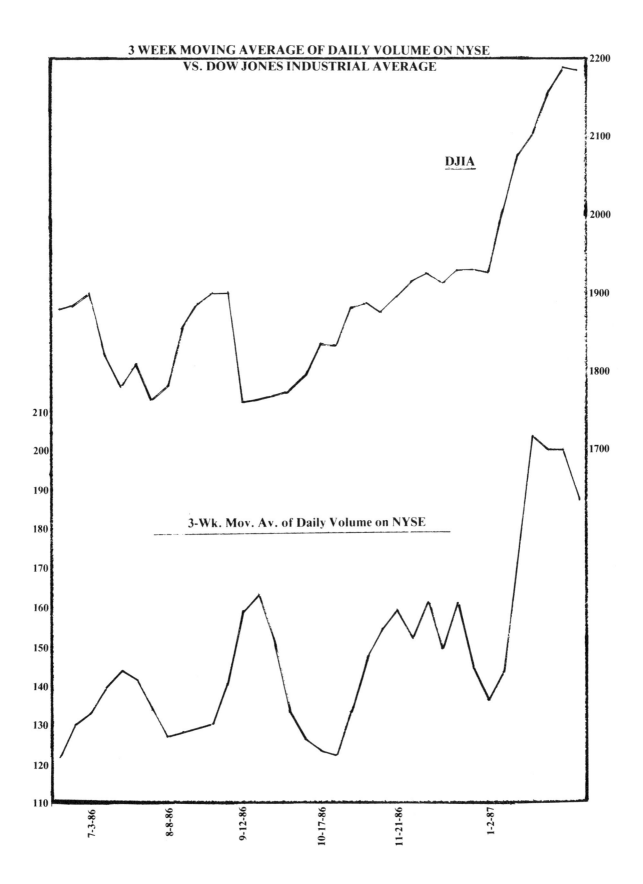

3 WEEK MOVING AVERAGE OF DAILY VOLUME ON NYSE
VS. DOW JONES INDUSTRIAL AVERAGE

DJIA

3-Wk. Mov. Av. of Daily Volume on NYSE

7-3-86 8-8-86 9-12-86 10-17-86 11-21-86 1-2-87

Chapter 8

Measuring the Volume Momentum
Or Volume Trend

In the previous chapter, we compared the level of trading volume with the changes in stock prices. This was done in relation to different points of time. Now, we turn to examine the influence of volume momentum on the general level of stock price. By volume momentum we mean the trend of volume, whether it be steadily rising, declining, or fluctuating within a narrow range over a period of time.

The trend of volume, as in the case of trend of stock price, can be gauged by the moving average method. For the measurement of volume trend or momentum we prefer to use a 10-week moving average of the average daily volume on NYSE.

To repeat, the 10-week moving average line shows the volume momentum, whereas the 3-week moving average, shown as dots in Figure 7-2, shows the current level of trading.

The interpretation of volume momentum can be summarized in a few statements as follows:

1. The 10-week moving average line depicts the volume momentum or trend.

2. Rising volume momentum is usually accompanied by rising prices, and conversely, falling volume trend is usually accompanied by declining prices.

3. When there is a disparity between volume trend and the trend of stock prices, the volume trend will usually foretell the movement of stock prices.

4. When the volume trend moves up and down in a low level of 70 to 90 million shares, the low level is more significant than the sidewise movement of the trend. As

said earlier, at this low level of volume, prices are usually falling and the immediate outlook is bearish.

5. When the 3-week moving average line penetrates the 10-week moving average line by more than 5% at the point of intersection, the prevailing volume trend may soon turn its direction.

REVIEW OF STOCK MARKET EXPERIENCE
JAN. 1982 TO JUNE 1986

Examination of Figure 7-2 yields the following observations:

1. The volume trend paralleled the stock price trend in 1982.

2. The volume trend showed earlier weakness in the first half of 1983, while stock prices continued to move up. In the second half of 1983, volume trend declined substantially at first and then recovered and moved up only mildly. The trend did not suggest good things for the stock market.

3. In the first two months of 1984, stock prices declined quickly, while the volume trend continued to move up. This is somewhat unusual. Beginning with March, however, volume trend moved down to parallel the trend in stock prices.

4. In January 1985, volume moved up sharply, stock prices followed, but not as strong as volume. Later, volume declined more than stock prices. In the second half of 1985, the pattern of volume trend was very similar to the trend of stock prices.

5. For the first 4 months of 1986, both the volume trend and stock price trend moved up sharply. However, at the beginning of May 1986 stock volume started to decline and yet stock price continued to rise. This disparity between volume trend and stock price trend suggested that there was a good probability the stock price may soon turn around and decline.

6. The overall record during the last 4½ years, except the first two months of 1984, seemed to fit quite well with what we outlined earlier regarding the general relationships between volume trend and movement in stock prices.

UP VOLUME VS.
DOWN VOLUME ON NYSE

Some technical analysts believe that the relationships between daily up volume and down volume and their trend are probably more meaningful than the total volume level and trend in foretelling future directions of the stock market.

In Table 7-1 we listed the average daily up volume and down volume on NYSE, the ratio between the two, and 3-week and 10-week moving averages of the ratio for the period from January 1982 to June 1986. The data is also charted in Figure 8-1. As we have done previously, we used the 10-week moving average of the ratio between up and down volume to denote the trend line.

Examination of Figure 8-1 yields the following observations:

1. The trendline of the ratio between up and down volume fluctuated more than the trendline of total volume on NYSE in 1982.

2. The trendline of the ratio between up and down volume declined earlier and more sharply in the last quarter of 1982 than the trendline of total volume on NYSE.

3. The trendline of the ratio between up and down volume in 1983 was similar to the trendline of total volume on NYSE.

4. The trendline of the ratio between up and down volume moved down in the first two months of 1984 in contrast to the trendline of the total volume on NYSE.

5. The trendline of the ratio between up and down volume fluctuated much more than the trendline of total volume on NYSE in 1985.

6. For the first six months of 1986, the pattern of the trendline of the ratio between up and down volume was very similar to the trendline of total volume. Again, the disparity between the trendline of the ratio of up volume to down volume and the trend in stock prices suggested there was a good possibility that stock price may soon start turning around and begin declining.

7. The overall record during 1982-1986 suggests that the trendline of the ratio between up and down volume is useful when it is evaluated together with the trendline of total volume on NYSE for indications of future trend in stock prices.

UPDATE—RECENT DEVELOPMENTS IN THE STOCK MARKET DURING THE PERIOD FROM JUNE 13, 1986 TO FEB. 13, 1987

To bring our readers up to date, I've prepared a chart on volume trend for the NYSE during the latest seven months, from June 1986 to Feb. 1987. Examination of the chart reveals the following:

1. Volume was going up from June 13 to Sept. 12, 1986. Volume was relatively

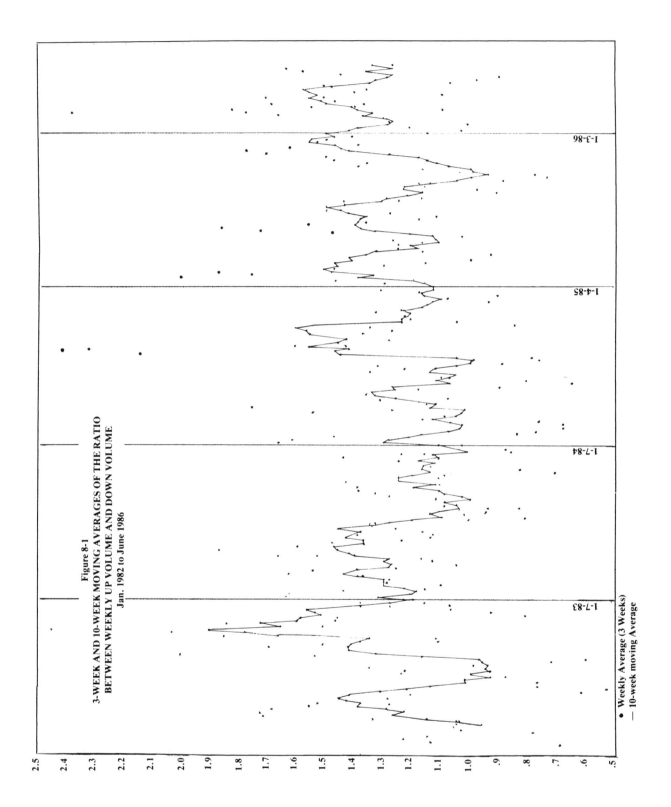

Figure 8-1
3-WEEK AND 10-WEEK MOVING AVERAGES OF THE RATIO
BETWEEN WEEKLY UP VOLUME AND DOWN VOLUME
Jan. 1982 to June 1986

● Weekly Average (3 Weeks)
— 10-week moving Average

stable during the next period, Sept. 12 to Nov. 28, 1986. Volume went up sharply from Nov. 28, 1986 to Feb. 13, 1987.

2. Volume trend over the whole seven months period was upward.

3. The stock price as measured by the DJIA did not respond to volume trend during the period from June 13 to Sept. 12, 1986. However, stock price since then moved up steadily through Feb. 13, 1987.

4. This recent experience confirmed what we said earlier about rising volume trend usually being accompanied by rising prices.

I've prepared another chart showing the ratio between up volume and down volume on NYSE over the latest seven months, from June 1986 to Feb. 1987.

The 3-week moving average shows the current level of the ratio between up volume and down volume, whereas the 10-week moving average shows the trend of this ratio. Examination of the chart shows the following:

1. The current level of the ratio shows wide fluctuation.

2. The trend of this ratio exhibits a similar pattern to that of the DJIA during the period from June 20 to Sept. 12, 1986. During the next period, from Sept. 12 to Jan. 2, 1987, the ratio showed a sidewise movement, whereas the DJIA moved gradually upward. Since Jan. 2, 1987 the trend of the ratio was upward and similar to the DJIA.

3. During the latest seven months, from June 1986 to Feb. 1987, the ratio between up volume and down volume did not add any new input of information about the future trend of stock prices.

4. The volume (or volume momentum) we discussed earlier in this chapter was a better indicator.

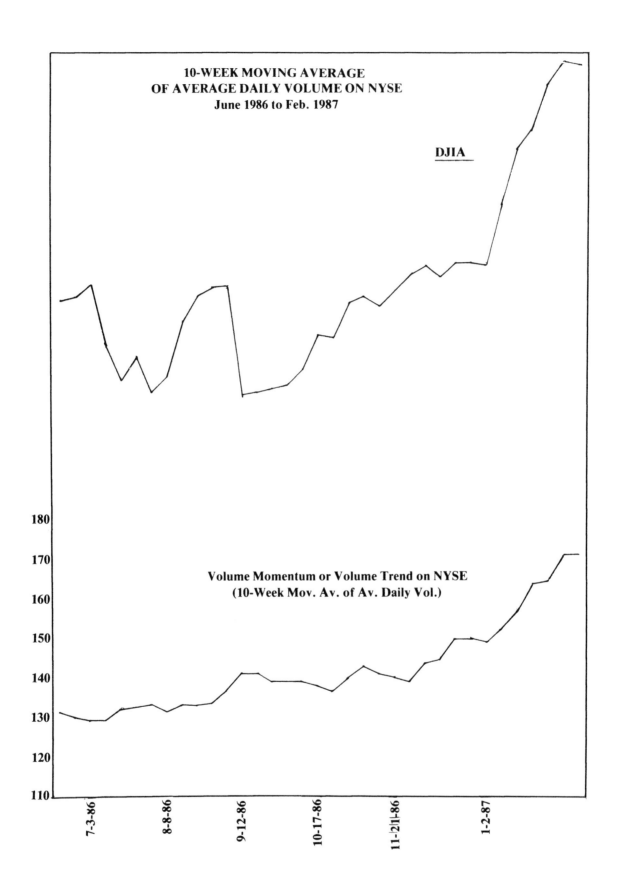

**10-WEEK MOVING AVERAGE
OF AVERAGE DAILY VOLUME ON NYSE
June 1986 to Feb. 1987**

DJIA

**Volume Momentum or Volume Trend on NYSE
(10-Week Mov. Av. of Av. Daily Vol.)**

180
170
160
150
140
130
120
110

7-3-86   8-8-86   9-12-86   10-17-86   11-21-86   1-2-87

3-WEEK AND 10-WEEK MOVING AVERAGES OF THE RATIO
BETWEEN WEEKLY UP VOLUME AND DOWN VOLUME
June 1986 to Feb. 1987

DJIA

10-Week Mov.Av. of the Ratio
Between Weekly Up Vol. and Down Vol.

3-Wk. Mov.Av. of the Ratio
Between Wkly. Up Vol. and Down Vol.

9-12-86

1-2-87

Chapter 9

Appraisal of Market Sentiment

Most experienced investors have observed and agreed that the stock market is moved by (1) real factors like earnings and dividends, and (2) investors' psychology at the moment. The latter sometimes can be more important than the former.

Mr. Walter Stone of Stone & Mead, Inc., an investment advisory firm in Boston prepared an interesting chart of the Cycle of Psychology in the stock market (see Figure 9-1).

The typical cycle of psychology in the stock market, Mr. Stone said, goes through these various stages:

1. *Deep Pessimism*
   Economic news is rapidly getting worse during this stage and investors feel that they should sell before any further sharp market decline.

2. *Disbelief*
   Economic news is still getting worse during this period, however there are rallies based on technical factors. At this point investors feel that this may be the last chance to sell before the decline resumes.

3. *Awakening*
   Economic news begins to improve during this period and the stock market gets a bit ahead of itself. Investors feel that they should wait for a reaction to buy.

4. *Belief*
   Economic news is improving rapidly with stocks going much higher. Investors feel that they should not wait for reactions to buy.

Figure 9-1
CYCLE OF PSYCHOLOGY

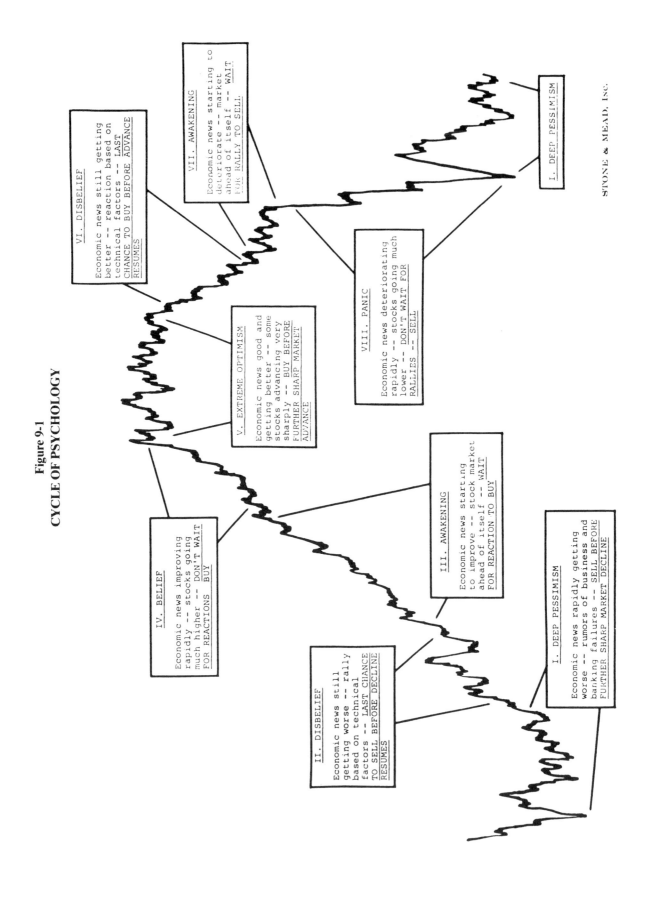

VI. DISBELIEF
Economic news still getting better -- reaction based on technical factors -- LAST CHANCE TO BUY BEFORE ADVANCE RESUMES

VII. AWAKENING
Economic news starting to deteriorate -- market ahead of itself -- WAIT FOR RALLY TO SELL

I. DEEP PESSIMISM

STONE & MEAD, INC.

V. EXTREME OPTIMISM
Economic news good and getting better -- some stocks advancing very sharply -- BUY BEFORE FURTHER SHARP MARKET ADVANCE

VIII. PANIC
Economic news deteriorating rapidly -- stocks going much lower -- DON'T WAIT FOR RALLIES -- SELL

IV. BELIEF
Economic news improving rapidly -- stocks going much higher -- DON'T WAIT FOR REACTIONS BUY

III. AWAKENING
Economic news starting to improve -- stock market ahead of itself -- WAIT FOR REACTION TO BUY

I. DEEP PESSIMISM
Economic news rapidly getting worse -- rumors of business and banking failures -- SELL BEFORE FURTHER SHARP MARKET DECLINE

II. DISBELIEF
Economic news still getting worse -- rally based on technical factors -- LAST CHANCE TO SELL BEFORE DECLINE RESUMES

5. *Extreme Optimism*

   Economic news is good and getting better with some stocks advancing very sharply. Investors feel that they should buy before any further sharp market advance.

6. *Disbelief*

   Economic news is still getting better, however there is some reaction in the stock market on the basis of technical factors. Investors feel that this may be the last chance to buy before the advance resumes.

7. *Awakening*

   Economic news begins to deteriorate and the stock market is choppy. Investors feel that they should wait for a rally to sell.

8. *Panic*

   Economic news is deteriorating rapidly and stocks are going much lower. Investors feel that they should not wait for rallies. They should sell.

9. *Deep Pessimism*

IMPORTANCE IN FINDING WAYS TO MEASURE MARKET SENTIMENT

Since market psychology plays a very important role in the movement of stock prices, it is obviously beneficial for both traders and non-traders to find ways to objectively measure the market sentiment at different points in time. Some of the useful ways of measuring market sentiment are discussed below.

MEASURING MARKET SENTIMENT BY PRICE/DIVIDEND RATIO (P/D RATIO)

Many experienced investors feel that the best way to measure market sentiment is by reference to price/dividend ratio. The P/D ratio does not fluctuate as much as the P/E ratio, because most corporations try to maintain a steady, or even better, a growing dividend payment.

The P/D ratio indicates how many dollars investors are willing to pay for $1 of dividends. The larger the P/D ratio, the greater the amount investors are willing to pay for $1 of dividends. If the P/D ratio is large, the investors must be bullish on the stock market, looking for more capital gain, or more dividend, or both. By the same token, if

Table 9-1
MEASURES OF OPTIMISM & PESSIMISM
IN THE STOCK MARKET

Yr.End Of Q		DJIA	12 Months Div.,DJIA	Price/Div. Ratio	Div. Yield on DJIA	Yield On 6M.Treas.Bill	Yield on Bill / Yield on DJIA
1986	T	1818.6	63.38	28.7	3.49	6.32%	1.81
1985	4	1546.7	62.03	24.9	4.01	7.09	1.77
	3	1328.6	61.83	21.5	4.65	7.27	1.56
	2	1335.5	61.53	21.7	4.61	7.16	1.55
	1	1266.8	61.56	20.6	4.86	8.92	1.84
1984	4	1211.6	60.63	20.0	5.00	8.36	1.67
	3	1206.7	58.41	20.7	4.84	10.51	2.17
	2	1132.4	57.67	19.6	5.09	10.55	2.07
	1	1164.9	56.39	20.7	4.84	9.58	1.98
1983	4	1258.9	56.33	22.3	4.47	9.14	2.04
	3	1233.1	54.59	22.6	4.43	9.19	2.07
	2	1222.0	54.05	22.6	4.42	8.89	2.01
	1	1130.0	54.10	20.9	4.79	8.33	1.74
1982	4	1046.5	54.14	19.3	5.17	8.23	1.59
	3	896.3	55.55	16.1	6.20	9.54	1.54
	2	811.9	55.84	14.5L	6.88	12.31	1.79
	1	822.8	56.28	14.6	6.84	12.62	1.85
1981	4	875.0	56.22	15.6	6.42	11.47	1.78
	3	850.0	56.18	15.1	6.61	15.06	2.28
	2	976.9	55.98	17.5	5.73	13.95	2.43
	1	1003.9	54.99	18.2	5.48	12.98	2.37
1980	4	964.0	54.36	17.7	5.64	14.77	2.62H
	3	932.4	53.83	17.3	5.77	10.55	1.83
	2	867.9	52.81	16.4	6.08	7.22	1.19
	1	785.8	52.10	15.1	6.63	15.10	2.28
1979	4	838.7	50.98	16.5	6.08	11.85	1.95
	3	878.7	51.45	17.1	5.86	10.13	1.73
	2	842.0	50.35	16.7	5.98	9.06	1.52
	1	862.2	49.48	17.4	5.74	9.46	1.65
1978	4	805.0	48.52	16.6	6.03	9.40	1.56
	3	865.8	47.42	18.3	5.48	7.95	1.45
	2	819.0	46.74	17.5	5.71	7.20	1.26
	1	757.4	46.53	16.3	6.14	6.64	1.08L
1977	4	831.2	45.84	18.1	5.51	6.38	1.16
	3	847.1	44.73	18.9	5.28	5.99	1.13
	2	916.3	43.85	20.9	4.79	5.20	1.09
	1	919.1	42.63	21.6	4.64	4.88	1.05
1976	4	1004.7	41.40	24.3	4.12	4.51	1.09
	3	990.2	38.90	25.5	3.93	5.31	1.35
	2	1002.8	38.10	26.3	3.80	5.78	1.52
	1	999.5	36.88	27.1	3.69	5.49	1.49
1975	4	852.4	37.46	22.8	4.39	5.93	1.35
	3	793.9	38.28	20.7	4.82	6.87	1.43
	2	879.0	38.66	22.7	4.40	5.46	1.24
	1	768.2	38.56	19.9	5.02	5.64	1.12
1974	4	616.2	37.72	16.3	6.12	7.09	1.16
	3	607.9	37.89	16.0	6.23	8.60	1.38
	2	802.4	36.82	21.8	4.59	8.23	1.79
	1	846.7	36.22	23.4	4.28	7.83	1.83
1973	4	850.9	35.33	24.1	4.15	7.44	1.79
	3	947.1	33.70	28.1	3.56	8.54	2.40
	2	891.7	33.10	26.9	3.71	7.23	1.95
	1	951.0	32.70	29.1H	3.44	6.43	1.87
Mean (1985-1973)				20.3			1.68

94

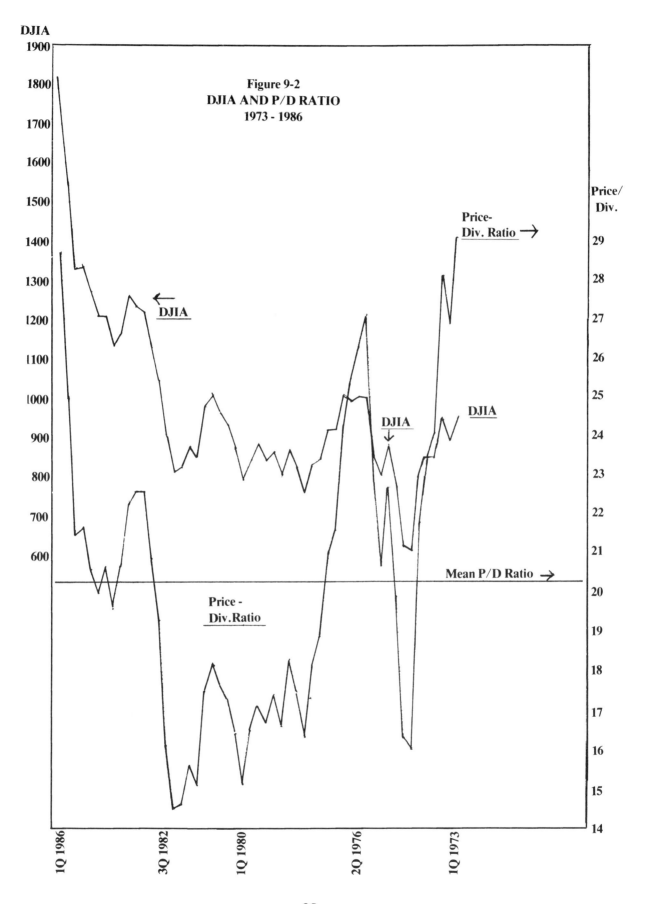

DJIA

Figure 9-2
DJIA AND P/D RATIO
1973 - 1986

Price/
Div.

Price-
Div. Ratio →

← DJIA

DJIA

DJIA

Mean P/D Ratio →

Price -
Div.Ratio

1Q 1986   3Q 1982   1Q 1980   2Q 1976   1Q 1973

95

the P/D ratio is low, investors must be wary about the stock market with the fear that the stock market will decline, bringing capital loss and/or a dividend cut.

Some experienced technicians believe that when the P/D ratio approaches 30, the stock market is facing trouble. To examine the historic record, we've prepared Table 9-1, showing the figures for DJIA, P/D ratio, and 12 months dividend for the period from the first quarter (1Q) 1973 to 1Q 1986. The data is also charted in Figure 9-2.

Looking over the record during the last 13 years, 1973 - 1986, we found the following:

1. The mean P/D ratio during the 13-year period was 20.3.

2. The high P/D ratio was 29.1 reached at the end of 1Q 1973, and the low was 14.5 reached at the end of 2Q 1982.

3. During the first three quarters of 1973, the P/D ratios were ranging from 26.9 to 29.1. Beginning with the 4th quarter, the market declined and reached a bottom of 607.9 at the end of 3Q in 1974.

4. During the first three quarters of 1976, the P/D ratios were ranging from 24.3 to 26.3, again moderately high by historical standards. The market declined in 1977 and reached a low of 757.4 at the end of 1Q 1978.

5. The P/D ratio fluctuated within a relatively low range of 15 to 18 most of the time during the years 1978 - 1982. The stock market was also sidewise most of the time during the same period.

6. The P/D ratio moved upward above 20 since 1Q 1983.

7. At the end of 4Q 1985, the P/D ratio reached 24.9, and at the end of 1Q 1986 the P/D ratio reached 28.7.

8. At this latest P/D ratio of 28.7, the technicians who believe in this ratio as a measure of market sentiment would probably conclude that the market sentiment was too high and that investors could expect a reaction in the market to take place soon.

MEASURING MARKET SENTIMENT BY THE RATIO BETWEEN THE YIELD ON TREASURY BILLS AND THE YIELD ON STOCKS IN DJIA

The price/dividend ratio to measure market sentiment, as was just discussed, is a logical approach. It's usefulness was proven by our examination of the experience in the stock market over the last 13 years. However, aside from measuring market sentiment, the P/D ratio is also affected by the level of current interest rates. Therefore, we propose another ratio to go with the P/D approach to measure market sentiment.

This ratio is obtained by dividing the current yield on six month Treasury Bills by the yield on the 30 stocks included in the DJIA (the yield on the DJIA is obtained by dividing the DJIA into its 12 months' dividend). If this ratio is 2.5, that means the yield on Treasury Bills is two and a half times the dividend yield on the DJIA. It also means that investors must be very bullish on the stock market, anticipating a rise in stock prices to bring in capital gains, or a dividend increase, or both. By the same token, if the ratio is one or less, it means that interest yield on Treasury Bills is the same or lower than the dividend yield on the DJIA. Investors would be bearish, not looking for a rise in stock prices or a dividend increase.

Table 9-1 shows the quarterly yield on six month Treasury Bills, the DJIA, its 12 months' dividend and the ratio between interest yield and stock yield. The data is also charted in Figure 9-3.

Looking over the experience over the last 13 years (1973 - 1986) as shown in the table and chart, we found the following:

1. The mean ratio between interest yield on six month Treasury Bills and the stock yield on DJIA during the 13 year period was 1.68.

2. The high of the ratio was 2.62 reached at the end of 4Q 1980, and the low was 1.08 reached at the end of 1Q 1978.

3. During the four years 1975 - 1978, the ratio was fluctuating within a low range of 1.1 to 1.5.

4. Since 1979, the trend of the ratio has been upward except the 2Q in 1980.

Now we compare the experience of both ratios, P/D and Y(bill)/Y(stocks), during the last 13 years (1973-1986). We found the following:

1. The stock market declined in 3Q1973 when the P/D ratio was high at 28.1 and the Yield(Bill)/Yield(Stocks) ratio was also high at 2.4.

2. At the end of 1Q 1976, P/D ratio was high at 27.1, but the Y(Bill)/Y(Stocks) ratio was at a moderately low level of 1.5. The DJIA was fluctuating sidewise during the next 4 quarters.

3. At the end of 4Q 1980, the Y(Bill)/Y(Stocks) ratio reached a high of 2.62, but the P/D ratio was at a moderate level of 17.7. The market did decline during the next 4 quarters, but only moderately.

4. At the end of 4Q 1983, the P/D ratio was at 22.3, about 10% higher than the average during the 13-year period, and the Y(Bill)/Y(Stocks) ratio was 2.04, about 20% higher than its average during the same period. The market did decline in the next two quarters to the extent of about 10%.

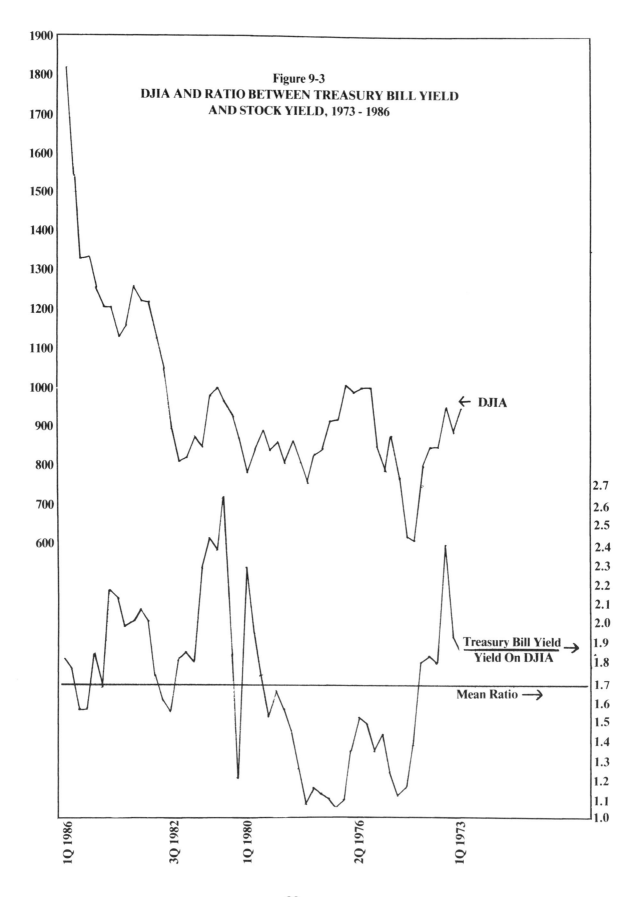

Figure 9-3
DJIA AND RATIO BETWEEN TREASURY BILL YIELD
AND STOCK YIELD, 1973 - 1986

98

5. Recently at the end of 1Q 1986, the P/D ratio reached 28.7, quite high by historical record, and yet the Y(Bill)/Y(Stocks) ratio was at 1.8, only slightly higher than its average of 1.68 over the last 13 year period.

6. The disparity between these two ratios at the end of 1Q 1986 suggested that the stock market was vulnerable. However, the Y(Bill)/Y(Stocks) ratio suggested only a moderate decline, whereas the P/D ratio would suggest a decline of larger proportions.

7. The review of the experience of the stock market in reference to these two ratios indicates that both ratios are useful in measuring market sentiment and foretelling future movements in stock prices. However, *a combined use of these two ratios at the same time* can provide better results in judging market sentiment and forecasting future movement in stock price.

MEASURING MARKET SENTIMENT
BY THE PROPORTION OF NYSE STOCKS
WHICH WERE ABOVE THEIR 10-WEEK MOVING AVERAGE

The 10-week moving average of stock prices, as we mentioned before, can be used to measure the immediate trend of stock prices. Investors Intelligence, a well known investment advisory firm, reports weekly on their diffusion index giving the percentage of NYSE stocks which are above their 10-week moving average.

According to their experience, when the diffusion index rises above 70%, 80%, or 90%, depending upon the strength of the upmove in progress, a termination of the upmove is signalled. Conversely, when the diffusion index dips below 30%, 20%, or 10%, depending upon the strength of the downmove, a termination of the downmove is indicated.

In Figure 9-4 you'll see a point and figure chart from Investors Intelligence showing the percentage of NYSE stocks above their 10-week moving average over a six year period from 1977 to 1982.

Figure 9-5 shows the percentage of NYSE stocks above their 10-week moving average since 1983.

The diffusion index, like rate of change analysis, leads the aggregate on both upturns and downturns. We feel this indicator is useful in measuring market sentiment and informing us how strong the current trend is, whether it's upward or downward, and when the current trend is most likely to terminate and turn around.

Figure 9-4

% OF NYSE STOCKS ABOVE THEIR 10-WEEK MOVING AVERAGE

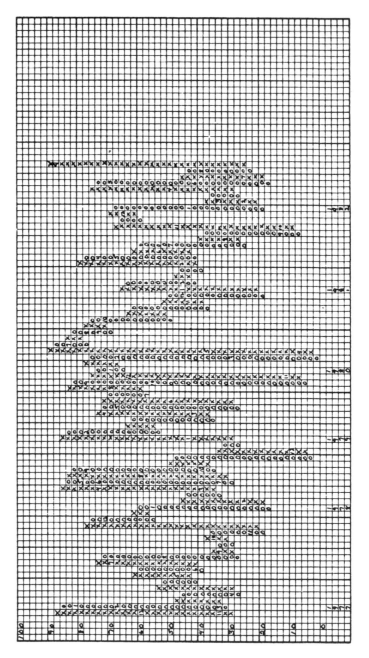

Source: Cohen, A. W., *How to Use the Three-Point Reversal Method of Point and Figure Stock Market Trading*, Investors Intelligence, 1982, p. 102.

100

Figure 9-5
% OF NYSE STOCKS ABOVE THEIR 10-WEEK MOVING AVERAGE

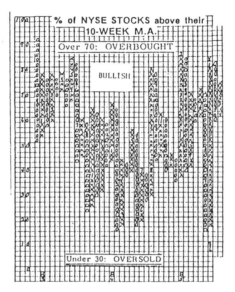

% of NYSE Stocks Above Their 10-Week Moving Average — This chart gives the % of NYSE stocks above their 10-week moving average. Above 70% the market may be considered to be overbought; below 30% the market may be considered to be oversold.

Source: *Point & Figure Chart Book,* Investors Intelligence, March 1986.

MEASURING MARKET SENTIMENT
OF THE GENERAL PUBLIC

We've just discussed three different methods to measure the overall market sentiment. Now, we turn to measuring market sentiment of special groups of investors and investment professionals.

First, we take the general public. The net subscriptions (subscriptions less redemptions) of mutual funds represent the general public's net demand for mutual funds, which invest most of their funds in stocks. The net subscription of mutual funds is, therefore, a good indicator of the market sentiment of the general public.

Figure 9-6 shows the DJIA and the net subscriptions of member funds of the Investment Company Institute for the period from 1977 to 1986.

As shown in the chart, from 1977 to 1982 there was practically no net subscription to mutual funds. The public was unenthused about the stock market during those years.

In 1983 there was a sharp increase in the net subscription of mutual funds. However, in 1984 the public returned to the sidelines. In 1985, the net subscriptions of the general public rose from a level of $20 billion at the beginning of the year to over $90 billion by the year's end. The stock market exhibited a pattern very similar to the net subscription of mutual funds, with only minor variations.

MEASURING THE MARKET SENTIMENT
OF MUTUAL FUNDS BY THEIR CASH RATIO

Mutual funds have to maintain certain amounts of liquid funds for redemptions by shareholders. In addition, they also vary the amount of cash funds in relation to the outlook of the stock market.

From 1977 to 1986 the ratio of liquid funds to total assets of mutual funds ranged from 6½% to 11½% with a mean of 9% as shown in Chart 9-7.

If the ratio is close to the high side of the historic range, it means that mutual funds as a group are not very optimistic about the stock market. On the other hand, if the ratio is close to the low side of the historic range, it means mutual funds are quite optimistic about the stock market.

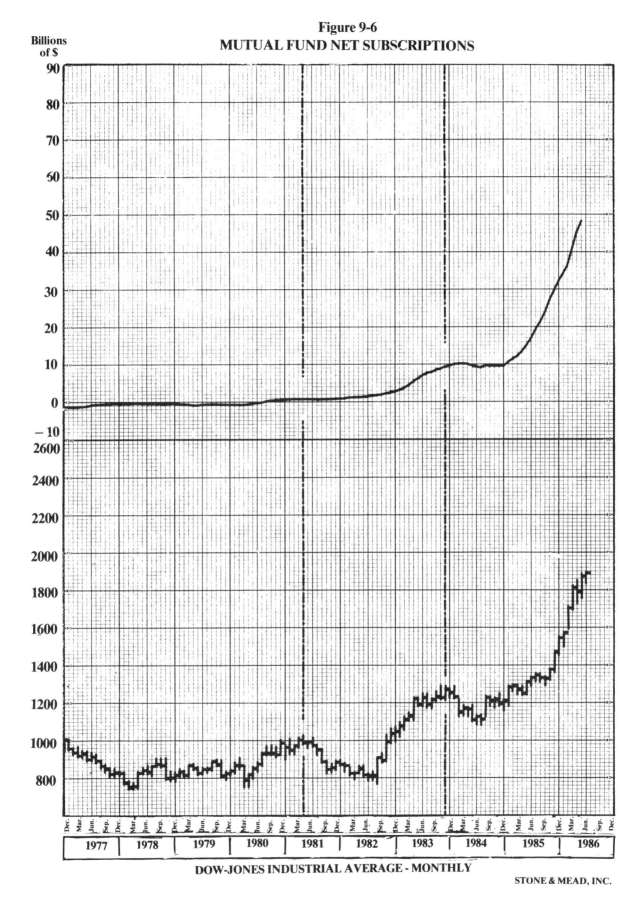

Figure 9-6
MUTUAL FUND NET SUBSCRIPTIONS

Billions
of $

DOW-JONES INDUSTRIAL AVERAGE - MONTHLY

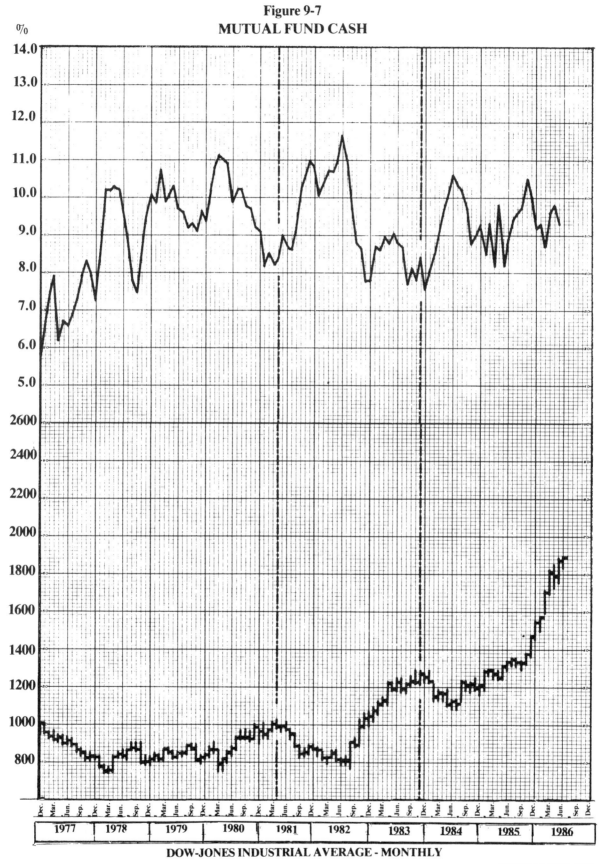

Figure 9-7
MUTUAL FUND CASH

%

DOW-JONES INDUSTRIAL AVERAGE - MONTHLY

STONE & MEAD, INC.

104

MEASURING MARKET SENTIMENT OF SPECIALISTS
ON NYSE BY THEIR SHORT SALES RATIO

Specialists on the New York Stock Exchange are charged with the responsibility of maintaining an orderly market in the stocks for which they serve as specialists.

When there is a temporary gap between buy orders and sell orders, specialists are required to step in to purchase or sell from their inventory of stocks so that the changes in stock prices will be orderly and gradual, either on the upside or the downside.

Specialists represent a group of knowledgeable and sophisticated investment professionals. Their trading activity is closely watched by the Securities and Exchange Commission (SEC), the NYSE itself, and investors in general. Weekly data on trading activity of the specialists are published by the SEC, but with a two week lag.

Since specialists are considered by many to be sophisticated investment professionals, their short sale ratio (short sales of specialists divided by total short sales) is closely watched by the investment community. When their short sales volume rises relative to the total short sale volume on NYSE (meaning rising short sale ratio), specialists are bearish and it is more likely that stock prices will subsequently decline. Conversely, when the specialists cut back on their short selling, the implication is that they are more bullish than other short sellers, and the market will likely advance in the near future.

Norman Fosback did an empirical study on the market performance of the short sales ratio of the specialists. During the 35 years from 1941 to 1975, the results, he reported, were these:

Specialist Short Sales Ratio (SS/TS)	S&P 500 Index One Year Later	Probability Of Rising Prices
Under 45%	+ 17.1%	84%
45% to 50%	+ 10.6%	72%
50% to 55%	+ 6.7%	70%
55% to 60%	+ 3.7%	59%
Over 60%	+ 0.4%	54%
35 Year Average	+ 7.7%	68%

Fosback concluded that the study did prove that specialists as a group were quite sophisticated in selling short and that the short selling ratio of the specialists, when below 45%, was a good bullish indicator.

Figure 9-8, prepared by Stone & Mead, Inc., shows the experience of specialists' short sale ratio and the DJIA for the last 10 years. The range of the short-sales ratio of the specialists was from a low of 33 to a high of 48. The mean was around 40. On the basis of what was experienced during the last 10 years, when the ratio moves above 45%, it is unfavorable and may signal a market top. On the other hand, when the short-sales ratio declines below 40%, the market may not be far from the bottom.

MEASURING THE MARKET SENTIMENT OF INVESTMENT ADVISORS

Investors Intelligence publishes an index known as the Advisory Sentiment Index. This index measures the percentage of investment advisory services which are bearish. Since most advisory services are trend followers, they are most bearish at market bottoms and least bearish at market tops. So this is a reverse indicator, which means when a great majority of advisory services are bearish, the stock market is bullish, and when a great majority of advisory services are bullish, the stock market is bearish.

The index has a good track record over the last 10 years and we feel the indicator will continue to be useful in the future as long as the majority of advisory services remain trend followers, which is quite probable.

Figure 9-9 shows the Bearish Sentiment Index (reported by Investors Intelligence) for the period from December 1983 to September 1984. Notice the scale for the index is on the left side with the low percentages at the top and high percentages at the bottom. The DJIA is measured by the scale on the right side in the chart.

CONCLUDING REMARKS:

In this chapter, we first examined methods to measure overall market sentiment. We introduced three methods: (1) P/D ratio, (2) Bill Yield/Stock Yield ratio, and (3) % of stocks over their 10-week moving average.

Then, we discussed methods to measure market sentiment of particular groups of investors and investment professionals. We discussed market sentiment of four groups:

1. **General Public:** by net increase of subscriptions to mutual funds.
2. **Mutual Funds:** by liquid funds ratio of mutual funds.
3. **Specialists on NYSE:** by their short sales ratio.
4. **Investment Advisors:** by Advisory Sentiment Index reported by Investors Intelligence, Inc.

106

Figure 9-8
SPECIALIST'S SHORT SALE RATIO

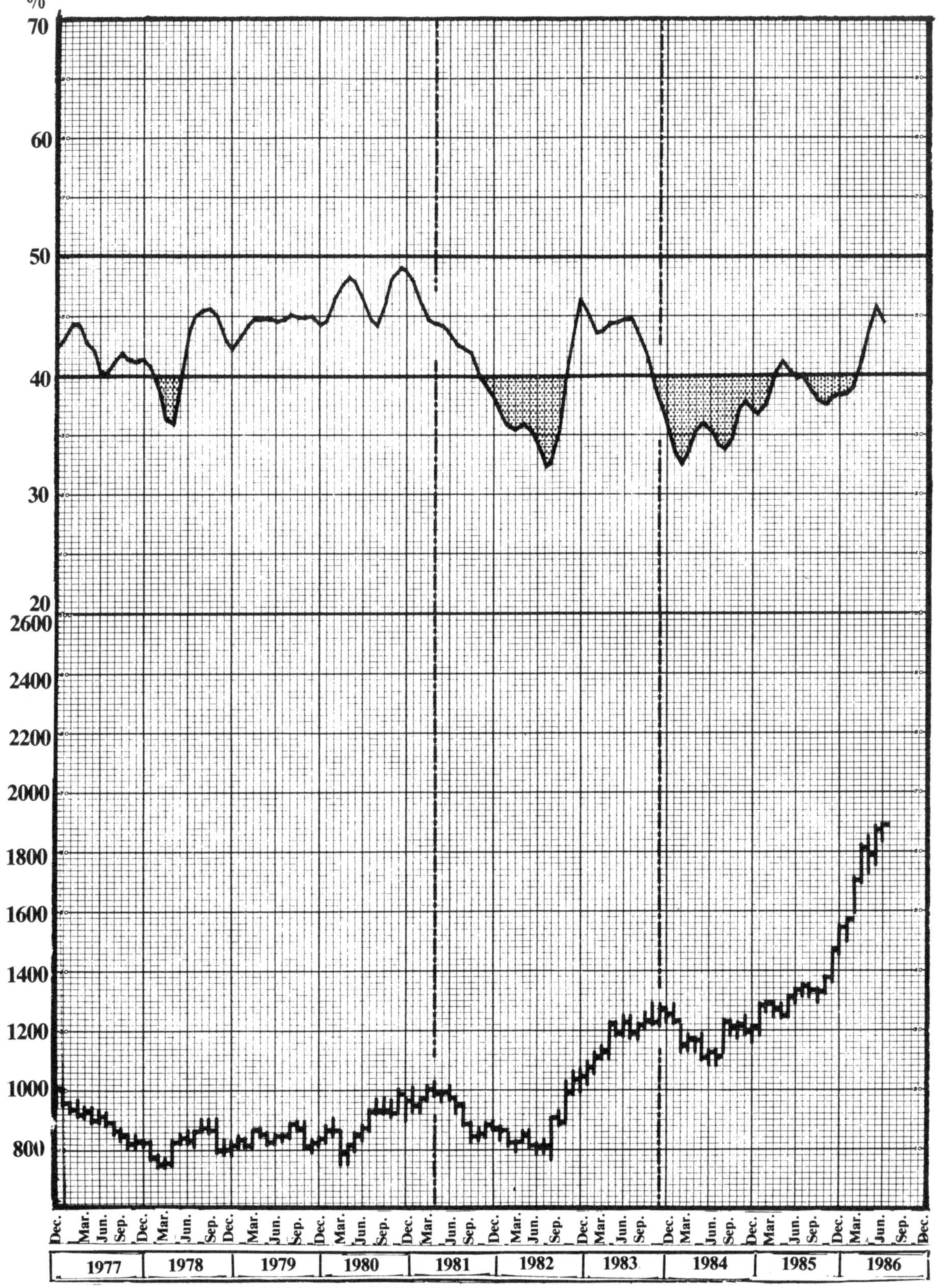

DOW-JONES INDUSTRIAL AVERAGE — MONTHLY

STONE & MEAD, INC.

107

Figure 9-9
BEARISH SENTIMENT INDEX

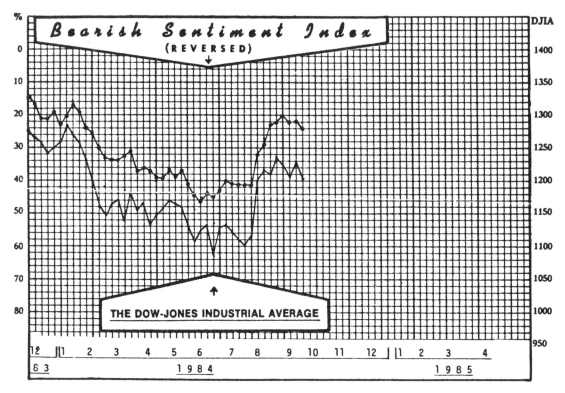

Source: *Investors Intelligence,* Sept. 28, 1984

108

In terms of relative importance, we prefer to give more weight to the overall market sentiment indicators, particularly the first two ratios: P/D and Bill Yield/Stock Yield.

The measurements of particular groups of investors and investment professionals are both logical and useful. The measurements discussed here covered important groups of investors and professionals. However, we prefer to use them as confirming evidence of the overall market sentiment. In other words, we are inclined to lean more on overall market sentiment and only secondarily on the sentiment indicators of particular groups.

Chapter 10

Appraisal of Other Indicators

Some technical analysts and technical advisory services are reported to follow as many as 50 to 70 technical indicators. We are not in favor of this approach because when a service is following 50 to 70 indicators without classifying and weighing them, it can create a "lost in the forest" effect on the investor.

Many indicators will undoubtedly duplicate one another without adding any new information. Some indicators are more important than others, and should not be treated indiscriminately with others. Out of a total of 50 to 70 indicators, many will turn out favorable, many unfavorable, and many neutral. This makes it very difficult to interpret and get the correct "message" from these indicators.

A second problem lies in the specific indicators which many analysts and services use. Many of the indicators depend on receiving market data including the high and the low, however the system of reporting new high and new low data has an important drawback. A new high is reported when a stock hits a new high anytime during the day, but actually the price of the stock can be lower than the previous day at closing. The same system of reporting applies also to a new low.

The new high and new low data in the past were usually found to lag behind the turning points of a market cycle. That is, at market top we often saw that there were many new highs, and at market bottom there were many new lows. The new high and new low numbers were, therefore, really lagging rather than leading indicators.

111

CONTROVERSY ABOUT THE VALIDITY
OF THE SHORT INTEREST THEORY

One of the technical theories which has a wide following in Wall Street is the short interest theory. The theory runs like this: a rising volume of short interest or a rising short interest ratio (short interest divided by average daily volume of transactions) is bullish, because the short seller will eventually buy back the stock he sold short. The short interest represents latent demand. The greater the short interest, the more likely is it that the price of the security will go up. Conversely, declining short interest and short interest ratio would be bearish.

Though this theory has been widely held among technicians and investors, many analysts question the validity of the theory. They point out that there are three different types of short selling: (1) shorts by investors believing in fundamental factors, (2) shorts by investors on basis of technical analysis, and (3) shorts by investors for tax reasons. Each type of short is different in terms of intention and the timing of cover and, therefore, their influences would not be the same.

The empirical findings from carefully made studies also found mixed results for the short interest theory.

In addition, new financial instruments introduced in the last 15 years have changed the behavior of investors and further clouded the validity of the short interest theory. The introduction of options on individual stocks, options on market indexes, and futures on market indexes have provided the possibility of new financial strategies and more flexibility in risk adjustments of investors' portfolios. Individual and institutional investors can now short in one market and hedge the short in another market.

The rise of a short-interest figure, therefore, does not necessarily mean that short-sellers or investors in general are becoming more bearish, because the increase in short-interest can be offset or more than offset by countervailing action in other markets.

A USEFUL TOOL—
OBSERVATION OF "ODD LOT ACTIVITY"

In the distant past, odd-lotters (those who purchase less than 100 shares) may not have been as marketwise as round lotters. However, I do not believe that to be the case today. Figure 10-1 shows the ratio of odd lot purchases to sales and DJIA in the last 10 years. The ratio ranged from a low of 0.32 to a high of 0.56 with a mean of 0.44. From the chart, we can see that the odd lotters began buying aggressively at the end of 1982

Figure 10-1
RATIO OF ODD LOT PURCHASES TO SALES—
PLOTTED INVERSELY

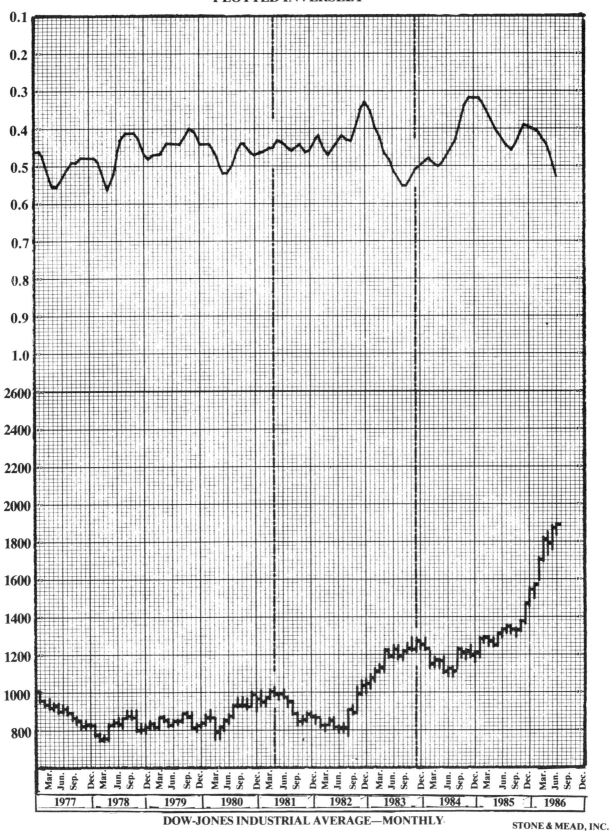

DOW-JONES INDUSTRIAL AVERAGE—MONTHLY

STONE & MEAD, INC.

113

and again at the end of 1Q 1985. Beginning with 3Q 1983, they began to cut down their purchases and continued to pare down their purchases in 1984. These timing decisions by the odd lotters proved to be quite good in terms of subsequent movements in stock prices.

OTHER USEFUL INDICATORS

Degree of Speculations in the Stock Market

From past experience we know that the stock market is highly emotional. It alternates between over-enthusiasm and over-pessimism. In time of over-enthusiasm there is usually wide speculation, especially in small, little known speculative issues. The degree of speculative fever in the marketplace is, therefore, a good barometer indicating whether the general market is relatively sound, depressed, or reaching dangerous proportions.

There are different ways of measuring speculative fever in the marketplace. We prefer to measure the degree of speculation in the stock market by the ratio that NASDAQ volume is as a % to NYSE volume.

Chart 10-2 shows NASDAQ volume relative to NYSE volume for the last four years (1983 - 1986). From the chart, we can readily see that the stock market has already developed some speculative fever in the first half of 1986.

Figure 10-2
NASDAQ VOLUME AS % OF NYSE VOLUME

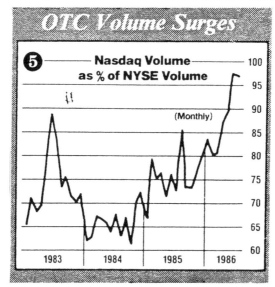

Source: *Barron's* July 7, 1986

114

Disparity of Price Movement Among DJIA, S&P's 500,
Value Line Composite and NASDAQ OTC Composite

Another useful indicator is the comparative movement of market indexes like the DJIA, S&P's 500, Value Line Composite, and NASDAQ OTC Composite. Usually the DJIA and S&P's 500 go together, because DJIA represents 30 blue-chip stocks, and the S&P's 500 is a weighted average also dominated by big blue-chips. On the other hand, the Value Line Composite is a strict unweighted average. It gives each stock the same weighting and includes all the issues (about 1700). It reflects the average performance of the overall market.

Figure 10-3
VALUE LINE COMPOSITE VS. DJIA

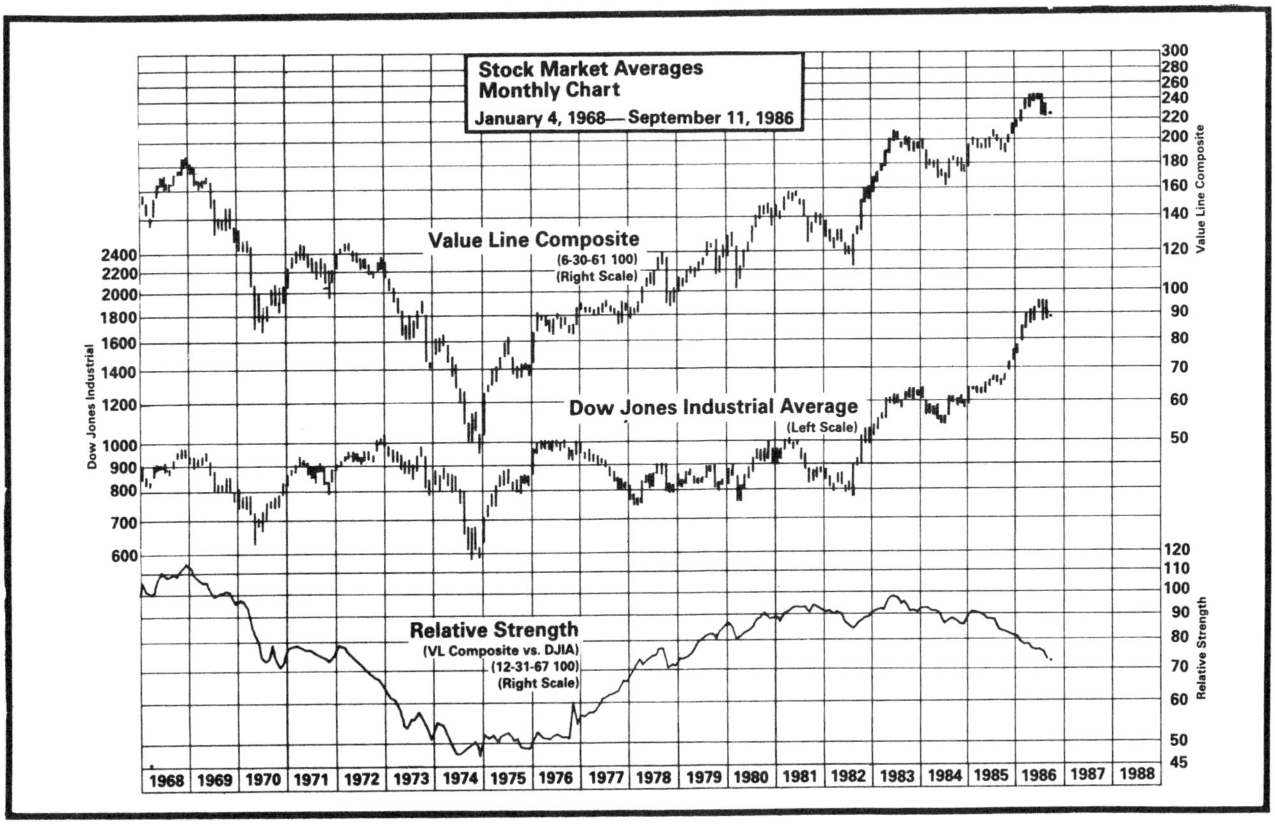

Source: Value Line *Selection & Opinion,* July 11, 1986.

Figure 10-3 shows the Value Line Composite, DJIA and the relative strength of the Value Line Composite (VLC as % of DJIA). If the relative strength line is moving up, that means the VLC is increasing faster than the DJIA (or declining slower than the DJIA). Conversely, if the VLC is moving down, it means the DJIA is increasing faster than the VLC. The relative strength line can, therefore, be looked upon as an indicator of disparity between the DJIA and the VLC.

In the year and a half from January 1985 to June 1986, the relative strength line of the VLC moved down steadily. This raised the question of whether the DJIA would be able to continue to move up for long without the overall market fully participating in the upmove.

A chart similar to Figure 10-3 could be prepared between the DJIA and the NASDAQ OTC Composite. The relative strength line between those two indexes would show whether there was substantial disparity between them at the moment. We feel this disparity indicator is a very useful technical indicator.

Call Volume, Put Volume,
And Their Rate of Turnover

The activity of speculators in the options markets should provide a useful source of information and make a good technical indicator. When speculators are bullish, they should be expected to buy more calls and less puts. Conversely, when they are bearish, they should buy more puts and less calls.

In Table 10-1, we include the activity of speculators in buying calls and puts on the Chicago Board (CBO) for the period from January 1984 to July 1986. We explain the data in the table as follows:

1. Column 1 shows the total weekly volume of calls on CBO.
2. Column 2 shows the weekly open interest of calls (calls outstanding for each week) on CBO.
3. Column 3 shows the turnover of calls (call volume divided by open interest of calls) which indicates the weekly call volume per unit of calls outstanding.
4. Column 4 shows the total weekly volume of puts on CBO.
5. Column 5 shows the weekly open interest of puts (puts outstanding for each week) on CBO.
6. Column 6 shows the turnover of puts (puts volume divided by open interest of puts) which means the weekly volume of puts per unit of puts outstanding.
7. Column 7 shows the ratio of puts turnover to calls turnover. This ratio should be high when speculators are bearish, and conversely, this ratio should be low when they are bullish.

116

Table 10-1
CALL VOLUME, PUT VOLUME, OPEN INTEREST & TURNOVER
ON CHICAGO BOARD, Jan. 1984 to July 1986

	1	2	3	4	5	6	7	
Date	Call Volume	Open Interest	Turnover of Call 1/2	Put Volume	Open Interest	Turnover of Put 4/5	Put Turn. Call Turn. 6/3	DJIA
1983								
12-30	1298410	5677695	0.23	516844	1964872	0.26	1.13	1258.6
1984								
1-6	1380054	5496894	0.25	442938	2002359	0.22L	0.88	1286.6
1-13	1287524	5646286	0.23	579700	2071411	0.28	1.22	1270.1
1-20	1431663	5653133	0.25	706166	2132750	0.33	1.32	1259.1
1-27	1243716	3902264	0.32	671696	1309186	0.51	1.59	1230.0
2-3	1427314	4124776	0.35	779817	1364278	0.57	1.63	1197.0
2-10	1457611	4456162	0.33	1137317	1432888	0.79	2.39	1160.7
2-17	1285943	4576257	0.28	928251	1431913	0.65	2.32	1148.9
2-24	975846	3643931	0.27	600717	1092187	0.55	2.04	1165.1
3-2	1314430	3896487	0.34	854564	1270592	0.67	1.97	1171.5
3-9	1268989	4106819	0.31	1001112	1336723	0.75	2.42	1139.8
3-16	1574659	4154034	0.38	911506	1484959	0.61	1.61	1184.4
3-23	952089	3374419	0.28	659565	1226624	0.54	1.93	1154.8
3-30	967076	3565903	0.27	532247	1311576	0.41	1.52	1164.9
4-6	1093249	3803969	0.29	915547	1370794	0.67	2.31	1132.2
4-13	1344374	4000808	0.34	1026714	1423846	0.72	2.12	1150.1
4-19	1058600	4057999	0.26	624121	1491346	0.42	1.62	1158.1
4-27	1125175	2935653	0.38	602371	1097331	0.55	1.45	1169.1
5-4	1394831	3160702	0.44	753067	1301509	0.58	1.32	1165.3
5-11	1403730	3454268	0.41	869017	1414427	0.61	1.49	1157.1
5-18	1394989	3595847	0.39	950008	1470037	0.65	1.67	1133.8
5-25	1250778	3377318	0.37	964137	1215894	0.79	2.14	1107.1
6-1	1122897	3594494	0.31	886639	1308995	0.68	2.19	1124.3
6-8	1337193	3862818	0.35	742510	1434355	0.52	1.49	1131.3
6-15	1331815	4027933	0.33	1249103	1446761	0.86H	2.60H	1086.9L
6-22	1520317	3381520	0.45	899075	1218995	0.74	1.64	1131.0
6-29	965437	3521464	0.27	626904	1311343	0.48	1.78	1132.4
7-6	621331	3667689	0.17L	459389	1364972	0.34	2.00	1122.6
7-13	1192639	3869959	0.31	917892	1353468	0.68	2.19	1109.9
7-20	1277345	3943665	0.32	903239	1402881	0.64	2.00	1101.4
7-27	1259486	3050910	0.41	751627	1063369	0.71	1.73	1114.6
8-3	2264832	3152456	0.72	917423	1231865	0.74	1.03	1202.1
8-10	2683747	3501555	0.77	954815	1509094	0.63	0.82L	1218.1
8-17	1533867	3637625	0.42	710812	1660767	0.43	1.02	1211.9
8-24	1377003	3358766	0.41	630995	1312779	0.48	1.17	1236.5
8-31	894106	3480520	0.26	453107	1411063	0.32	1.23	1224.4
9-7	1079037	3731443	0.29	538367	1476899	0.36	1.24	1207.4
9-14	1890428	3868922	0.49	909556	1581144	0.58	1.18	1237.5
9-21	1752828	4038328	0.43	962307	1688958	0.57	1.33	1201.7
9-28	1136981	3494609	0.33	678748	1318419	0.51	1.55	1206.7
10-5	1171113	3722705	0.31	773485	1360735	0.57	1.84	1182.5
10-12	1433666	4004212	0.36	808805	1401907	0.58	1.61	1190.7
10-19	2260272	4139132	0.55	864063	1490701	0.58	1.05	1225.9
10-26	1385960	3228058	0.43	580784	1041375	0.56	1.30	1205.0

117

Table 10-1 (Cont'd.)

	1	2	3	4	5	6	7	
Date	Call Volume	Open Interest	Turnover of Call 1/2	Put Volume	Open Interest	Turnover of Put 4/5	Put Turn. Call Turn. 6/3	DJIA
11-2	1361690	3499041	0.39	552121	1184286	0.47	1.21	1216.7
11-9	1668652	3812200	0.44	694437	1353187	0.51	1.16	1219.0
11-16	1637997	3930721	0.42	854066	1346935	0.63	1.50	1187.9
11-23	1046563	3094369	0.34	578555	1076407	0.48	1.41	1220.3
11-30	1405426	3341492	0.42	761115	1211385	0.63	1.50	1188.9
12-7	1461182	3721789	0.39	866365	1238300	0.70	1.79	1163.2
12-14	1344243	3786925	0.35	820053	1279935	0.64	1.83	1175.9
12-31	2363624	3914495	0.60H	910099	1413657	0.64	1.07	1199.0
12-28	614489	3140699	0.20	278338	1104935	0.25	1.25	1204.2
1985								
1-4	865971	3300530	0.26	500454	1183119	0.42	1.62	1185.0
1-11	1346031	3499784	0.38	591637	1254930	0.47	1.24	1218.1
1-18	2405011	3700524	0.65	832126	1484623	0.56	0.86	1227.4
1-25	2463891	2936580	0.84H	921712	1132756	0.81	0.96	1276.1
2-1	1981830	3253829	0.61	781259	1357592	0.58	0.95	1277.7
2-8	2035700	3484904	0.58	698819	1512624	0.46	0.79	1290.0
2-15	2370000	3707961	0.64	865312	1669845	0.52	0.81	1282.0
2-22	1185989	3244853	0.37	524856	1240565	0.42	1.14	1275.8
3-1	2156084	3562888	0.61	764624	1357638	0.56	0.92	1299.4
3-8	2004531	3793909	0.53	910842	1482975	0.61	1.15	1269.7
3-15	1680865	4060793	0.41	946776	1497651	0.63	1.54	1247.4
3-22	161581	3617172	0.45	788080	1250684	0.63	1.40	1267.5
3-29	1292129	3900938	0.33	615065	1338291	0.46	1.39	1266.8
4-4	1141629	4043246	0.28	562775	1412124	0.40	1.43	1259.0
4-12	1297632	4231278	0.31	681800	1478988	0.46	1.48	1265.7
4-19	1640924	4327299	0.38	759881	1531999	0.50	1.32	1266.6
4-26	1349403	3314810	0.41	638601	1082631	0.59	1.44	1275.2
5-3	1492725	3554689	0.42	797247	1188076	0.67	1.60	1247.2
5-10	1799226	3719963	0.48	777586	1257960	0.62	1.29	1274.2
5-17	2126188	3811049	0.56	776338	1338693	0.58	1.04	1285.3
5-24	1566661	3309351	0.47	644212	1148657	0.56	1.19	1302.0
5-31	1227165	3398690	0.36	494474	1233253	0.40	1.11	1315.4
6-7	1721616	3746749	0.46	696178	1407986	0.49	1.07	1316.4
6-14	1658314	3962155	0.42	1067324	1438582	0.74	1.76	1301.0
6-21	1823915	4263600	0.43	935862	1508402	0.62	1.44	1324.5
6-28	1681362	3697315	0.45	762427	1338604	0.57	1.27	1335.5
7-5	978111	3882264	0.25L	433416	1476109	0.29	1.16	1334.5
7-12	1457279	4113816	0.35	735573	1588625	0.46	1.31	1338.6
7-19	2325742	4230285	0.55	913105	1806895	0.51	0.93	1359.5
7-26	1546239	3463702	0.45	783636	1234471	0.63	1.40	1357.1
8-2	1385790	3725537	0.37	680154	1359759	0.50	1.35	1353.1
8-9	1371593	3954107	0.35	900087	1447795	0.62	1.77	1320.8
8-16	1423316	4173188	0.34	1095605	1475272	0.74	2.18	1312.7
8-23	1147003	3343654	0.34	671007	1147258	0.58	1.71	1318.3
8-30	917493	3579209	0.26	563051	1300904	0.43	1.65	1334.0
9-6	946100	3761966	0.25L	597879	1390909	0.43	1.72	1335.7
9-13	1642147	3960834	0.41	1301928	1457387	0.89H	2.17	1307.7
9-20	1542237	4210335	0.37	1325875	1504890	0.88	2.38H	1297.9
9-26	1317761	3542909	0.37	1052070	1327576	0.79	2.14	1320.8

118

Table 10-1 (Cont'd.)

	1	2	3	4	5	6	7	
Date	Call Volume	Open Interest	Turnover of Call 1/2	Put Volume	Open Interest	Turnover of Put 4/5	Put Turn. Call Turn. 6/3	DJIA
10-4	2155442	3566958	0.60	1279134	1401575	0.91	1.52	1328.7
10-11	1589094	4035086	0.39	969911	1579500	0.61	1.56	1339.9
10-18	2550214	4127482	0.62	1093450	1810635	0.60	0.97	1368.8
10-25	1496926	3289329	0.46	793652	1419250	0.56	1.22	1356.5
11-1	1697098	3505389	0.48	856285	1579500	0.54	1.13	1390.3
11-8	1940294	3650141	0.53	956174	1757302	0.54	1.02	1404.4
11-15	2987168	3823636	0.78	1293668	2081901	0.62	0.79	1435.1
11-22	1984694	3397285	0.58	885462	1566496	0.56	0.97	1464.3
11-29	1199491	3616166	0.33	512504	1715225	0.30	0.91	1470.0
12-6	2296620	3850940	0.60	1037651	1915432	0.54	0.90	1477.2
12-13	3366966	4101173	0.82	1171367	2155410	0.54	0.66L	1535.2
12-20	3102268	4294265	0.72	1212973	2437660	0.50	0.69	1543.0
12-27	994675	3727615	0.27	449462	1606795	0.28L	1.04	1543.0
1986								
1-3	1215776	3946273	0.31L	539195	1723954	0.31L	1.00	1549.2
1-10	2544683	4206303	0.60	1481331	1865499	0.79	1.32	1513.5
1-17	2018487	4394903	0.46	1051329	1994337	0.53	1.15	1536.7
1-24	1574926	3462247	0.45	990644	1320323	0.75	1.67	1529.9
1-31	2036455	3722003	0.55	1065740	1546864	0.69	1.25	1571.0
2-7	2292004	3934401	0.58	1243317	1784905	0.70	1.21	1613.4
2-14	2315164	4104151	0.56	1046950	2008065	0.52	0.93	1664.5
2-21	2737901	4139878	0.66	1103263	2234719	0.49	0.74L	1697.7
2-28	2316454	3656542	0.63	1092457	1679209	0.65	1.03	1709.1
3-7	2222949	4110582	0.54	1111373	1911564	0.58	1.07	1699.8
3-14	3116954	4304344	0.72H	1288797	2153960	0.60	0.83	1792.7
3-21	2796670	4473986	0.63	1170570	2413990	0.48	0.76	1768.6
3-28	1599709	3978755	0.40	755424	1640809	0.46	1.15	1821.7
4-4	2117106	4356863	0.49	1101812	1815580	0.61	1.24	1739.2
4-11	2626609	4655618	0.56	–	–	–	–	1790.2
4-18	2728763	4614801	0.59	1167983	2210893	0.53	0.90	1840.4
4-25	2117589	3812118	0.56	992313	1490034	0.67	1.20	1835.6
5-2	2174754	4198683	0.52	1110594	1676162	0.66	1.27	1774.7
5-9	1623114	4284744	0.38	789938	1849778	0.43	1.13	1789.4
5-16	2098902	4769189	0.44	1271377	1966366	0.65	1.48	1759.8
5-23	1767677	3870458	0.46	1026468	1481765	0.69	1.50	1823.3
5-30	1949768	4111527	0.47	1015063	1744492	0.58	1.23	1876.7
6-6	1668625	4283115	0.39	987980	1877891	0.53	1.36	1885.9
6-13	1985208	4451461	0.45	1242761	1991183	0.62	1.38	1874.2
6-20	2082742	4596564	0.45	999075	2099043	0.48	1.07	1879.5
6-27	1654956	3865047	0.43	807104	1501126	0.54	1.26	1885.3
7-3	1304135	4095481	0.32	613921	1671228	0.37	1.17	1900.9
7-11	2243172	4471925	0.50	1603956	1754613	0.91H	1.82H	1821.4

H: High for the year
L: Low for the year

119

The analysis of data in Table 10-1 yields the following statistics:

		Turnover of Call Volume	Turnover of Put volume	Put Turn. Call Turn.
1984	High	0.60	0.86	2.60
	Low	0.17	0.22	0.82
1985	High	0.84	0.89	2.38
	Low	0.25	0.28	0.66
1986 (1st hlf)	High	0.72	0.91	1.82
	Low	0.31	0.31	0.74
Average 1984-1986		0.43	0.57	1.40

The ratio of put turnover to call turnover and DJIA is also charted in Figure 10-4.

The average turnover of calls for the period 1984-1986 was 0.43. The turnover for puts was slightly higher at 0.57, and the average ratio between the turnover of puts and the turnover of calls was 1.40.

The DJIA declined about 15% in the first half of 1984 and recovered half of the loss in the second half of the year. The turnover of calls reached a low of 0.17 at the end of the week of July 6, 1984. The turnover of puts, on the other hand, reached a high for the year at 0.86 by June 15, 1986. The ratio of put turnover to call turnover reached a high for the year at 2.60, also by June 15, 1986.

The DJIA moved moderately upward in the first eight months of 1985, but really took off in the last four months of the year. The ratio of the turnover of puts to turnover of calls was below the average of 1.4 most of the time in the first half of 1985. In August and September of that year the ratio rose sharply, but the DJIA declined only moderately. Beginning with October, the ratio began to decline sharply until the end of the year, while the DJIA rose from 1300 to 1550 in the last three months of 1985.

The DJIA moved steadily upward in the first six months of 1986. The ratio of the put turnover to call turnover was below the average of 1.4 for 90% of the time during the first six months of 1986.

On an overall basis, the ratio of put turnover to call turnover behaved as we expected. When speculators are bearish, they would buy more puts than calls, and the ratio of put turnover to call turnover should be relatively high. Conversely, when speculators are bullish, the ratio should be relatively low.

Because the period we analyzed was relatively short, we cannot say whether the

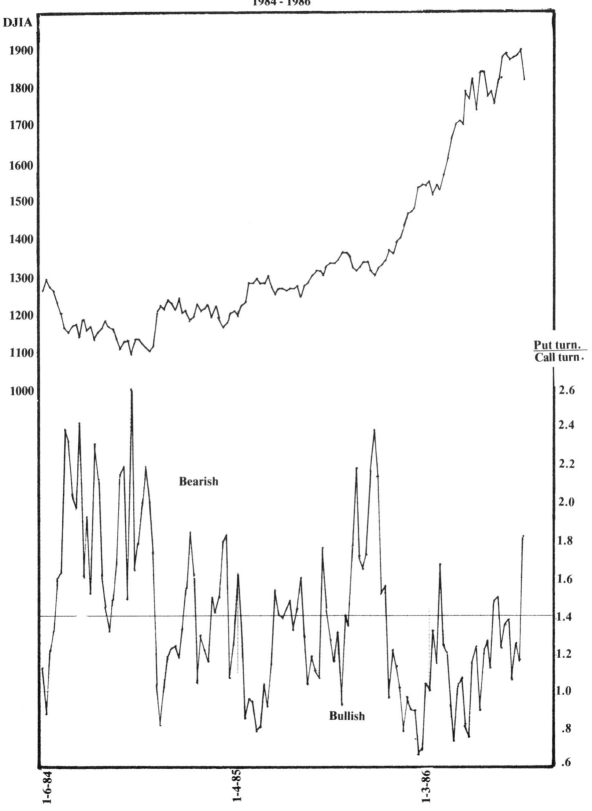

Figure 10-4
RATIO BETWEEN PUT TURNOVER, CALL TURNOVER, AND DJIA
1984 - 1986

DJIA

1900
1800
1700
1600
1500
1400
1300
1200
1100
1000

Put turn.
Call turn.

2.6
2.4
2.2
2.0
1.8
1.6
1.4
1.2
1.0
.8
.6

Bearish

Bullish

1-6-84   1-4-85   1-3-86

ratio of put turnover to call turnover is a leading or coinciding technical indicator. However, the information on the activity of speculation in the options markets is important, and serious traders and technicians should carefully look at this kind of data for good indicators.

In Table 10-1, we use the data of weekly total volume of calls and puts on CBO for analysis. Alternately, the weekly volume of calls and puts on S&P's 100 Index on CBO can be used to represent the speculative activity of traders in the options market.

Stock Index Futures

The trading of stock index futures began in 1982. Now, sophisticated investors and institutions can use the futures to speculate on stock price movement or hedge their portfolios.

When the future index sells above the current level of the stock index, the amount which exceeds the current index is known as the premium. On the other hand, when the future index sells below the current level of the index, the difference between the two is known as the discount.

The normal relationships between the current stock index and the future stock index (during a given duration) depend on two factors:

1. The first factor is the difference between financing the cost of the stock purchase and the yield of the stock dividend. Assume we use the yield on 6 month Treasury Bills to represent financing cost. The greater the amount that the yield on Treasury Bills exceeds the yield from the stock dividend, the higher would be the premium on the future stock index. That's because in order to induce people to hold stocks and sell the future index on them, they need to at least break even between financing costs and current income from stocks (stock dividend).

2. The second factor is the expectation of what the future stock price will be relative to the current price. If speculators are expecting a sharp rise in stock prices, the future stock index should sell at a high premium, and vice-versa. If this second factor is neutral (you expect no price change in stocks), then the premium is dependent totally on the first factor (the difference between financing cost and the yield from the stock dividend).

Normally, we should expect that the future index would sell higher than the current stock index, and that the longer the duration of the future stock index, the higher would be the premium. When the premium disappears, or becomes

122

negligible, it means speculators in the futures market are bearish. When a discount is evident in the future stock index, it means speculators are very pessimistic about the future stock price.

The spread between the current stock index and the future stock index is a very sensitive indicator. It changes very quickly. Therefore, this is a very short-term indicator. It is useful to help forecast what the market will probably do in the hours and days ahead.

For example, on Tuesday, July 22,1986 it was reported in The New York Times that the quotations of S&P's 500 Stock Index Futures finished the previous day as follows:

	Close	**Change**
Sept.	236.25	− .60
Dec.	238.15	− .45
March	240.00	− .40
June	241.90	− .40
Last Index	236.22,	off .15

The last index represents the current level of the S&P's 500 Index. There was almost no difference between the current level of the index and the September future index. That means, speculators were still bearish on stock prices for the next few weeks to two months.

Chapter 11

Appraisal of Monetary Environment

The changes and direction of interest rates can affect the prices of common stocks in three important ways:

1. The change in interest rates can affect general business conditions and corporate profitability and, therefore, dividends and prices of common stocks.

2. The changes in interest rates affect the relationship between the yield on bonds and the dividend yield of stocks and, therefore, the relative attractiveness of stocks vs. bonds.

3. The changes in interest rates affect the psychology of investors in relation to equity investment and, therefore, stock prices.

Many technical analysts include interest rates and Federal Reserve policy (which affects bank reserves and interest rates) as important technical indicators. Here we enter into the gray area between technical analysis and fundamental analysis. Theoretically, interest rates and Federal Reserve policy are fundamental factors which cause movements in security prices and, therefore, belong to the domain of fundamental analysis. The impact from changes in interest rates and Federal Reserve policy would be reflected in the marketplace in changes in volume of traded securities and changes in prices of securities.

We do not object to the inclusion of interest rates as a technical indicator. However, they should be treated as confirming evidence with changes in volume and prices of securities.

DISCOUNT RATE, RATE ON FEDERAL FUNDS
AND YIELD ON TREASURY BILLS

Short-term interest rates are more sensitive than long-term interest rates to changes in expectation of inflation, Federal Reserve policy, and shifts in demand and supply of funds in financial markets. Among the short-term interest rates, the most important and sensitive rates are these:

1. Discount rate which is charged by Federal Reserve Banks on borrowings of member banks from the Federal Reserve.

2. Federal Funds' rates which are the rates banks charge to each other on day to day loaning of excess reserves within the Federal Reserve System.

3. The yield on three month Treasury Bills.

Table 11-1 includes data on Federal Reserve discount rates, Federal Funds' rates, and the yield on three-month Treasury Bills for the period from January 1980 to June 1986. The analysis of the data in the table provides us the following findings:

1. The reduction of the discount rate which represents easing of monetary policy is usually favorable to the stock market. When reduction of discount rates is made several times over a short period of time, the stimulation to the stock market is particularly powerful. A good case in point would be the Autumn of 1982 when the Federal Reserve reduced the discount rate six times in a period of six months. The stock market responded with about a 50% rise in the next 12 months.

2. The Federal Reserve often claims that they adjust the discount rate to the market yield on Treasury Bills. The average difference between the discount rate and the yield on 3-month Treasury Bills for the period from January 1980 to June 1986 was about 0.05%. The small difference between the two rates does not necessarily prove the Federal Reserve's contention that the discount rate follows the yield on Treasury Bills. However, it does indicate to us that the difference between the two rates has been minor (about half a percent most of the time).

3. Federal Funds rate usually exceeded the discount rate. This is so because the Federal Reserve discourages banks from borrowing from the Federal Reserve. During the period from January 1980 to June 1986, the Federal Funds' rate on the average exceeded the discount rate by 1.23%. During the last quarter of 1980 and the first three quarters of 1981, when interest rates were high, the Federal Funds' rate exceeded the discount rate by as much as 5.9%. On the other hand, when the Federal Reserve was

Table 11-1
FEDERAL RESERVE DISCOUNT RATE, FEDERAL FUNDS RATE, AND YIELD ON THREE-MONTH TREASURY BILLS

Date Yr.Month		Federal Reserve Disc. Rate	Rate on Federal Funds	Yield on 3-Month Treas.Bills	Federal Funds in Excess of Disc.Rate	Disc. Rate in Excess of Yield on Treas.Bills	DJIA
1980	1	12	13.82	12.04	1.82	−0.04	875.9
	2	13	14.13	12.81	1.13	0.19	863.1
	3	13	17.19	15.53	4.19	−2.53	785.8
	4	13	17.61	14.0	4.61	−1.0	817.1
	5	13	10.98	9.15	−2.02	3.85	850.9
	6	12	9.47	7.0	−2.53	5.0	867.9
	7	11	9.03	8.13	−1.97	2.87	935.3
	8	10	9.61	9.26	−0.39	0.74	932.6
	9	11	10.87	10.32	−0.13	0.68	932.4
	10	11	12.81	11.58	1.81	−0.58	924.5
	11	12	15.85	13.89	3.85	−1.89	993.3
	12	13	18.9	15.66	5.90	−2.66	964.0
1981	1	14	19.08	14.72	5.08	−0.72	947.3
	2	14	15.93	14.91	1.93	−0.91	974.6
	3	14	14.70	13.48	0.70	0.52	1003.9
	4	14	15.72	13.64	1.72	0.36	997.8
	5	14	18.52	16.30	4.52	−2.30	991.8
	6	14	19.10	14.56	5.10	−0.56	976.9
	7	14	19.04	14.70	5.04	−0.70	952.3
	8	14	17.82	15.61	3.82	−1.61	881.5
	9	14	15.87	14.95	1.87	−0.95	850.0
	10	14	15.08	13.87	1.08	0.13	852.6
	11	13	13.31	11.27	0.31	1.73	889.0
	12	12	12.37	10.93	0.37	1.07	875.0
1982	1	12	13.22	12.41	1.22	−0.41	871.1
	2	12	14.78	13.78	2.78	−1.78	824.4
	3	12	14.68	12.49	2.68	−0.49	822.8
	4	12	14.94	12.82	2.94	−0.82	848.4
	5	12	14.45	12.15	2.45	−0.15	819.5
	6	12	14.15	12.11	2.15	−0.11	811.9
	7	11.5	12.59	11.91	1.09	−0.41	808.6
	8	10.5	10.12	9.01	−0.38	1.49	901.3
	9	10	10.31	8.20	0.31	1.80	896.3
	10	9.5	9.71	7.75	0.21	1.75	991.7
	11	9	9.20	8.04	0.20	0.96	1039.3
	12	8.5	8.95	8.01	0.45	0.49	1046.5
1983	1	8.5	8.68	7.81	0.18	0.69	1075.7
	2	8.5	8.51	8.13	0.01	0.37	1112.6
	3	8.5	8.77	8.36	0.27	0.14	1130.0
	4	8.5	8.80	8.25	0.30	0.25	1226.2
	5	8.5	8.63	8.19	0.13	0.31	1200.0

Table 11-1 (Cont'd.)

Date Yr.Month		Federal Reserve Disc.Rate	Rate on Federal Funds	Yield on 3-Month Treas.Bills	Federal Funds in Excess of Disc.Rate	Disc. Rate in Excess of Yield on Treas.Bills	DJIA
1983	6	8.5	8.98	8.82	0.48	−0.32	1222.0
	7	8.5	9.37	9.12	0.87	−0.62	1199.2
	8	8.5	9.56	9.39	1.06	−0.89	1216.2
	9	8.5	9.45	9.05	0.95	−0.55	1233.1
	10	8.5	9.48	8.71	0.98	−0.21	1225.2
	11	8.5	9.34	8.71	0.84	−0.21	1276.0
	12	8.5	9.47	8.96	0.97	−0.46	1258.6
1984	1	8.5	9.56	8.93	1.06	−0.43	1220.6
	2	8.5	9.59	9.03	1.09	−0.53	1154.6
	3	8.5	9.91	9.44	1.41	−0.94	1164.9
	4	9.0	10.29	9.69	1.29	−0.69	1170.8
	5	9.0	10.32	9.90	1.32	−0.90	1104.9
	6	9.0	11.06	9.94	2.06	−0.94	1132.4
	7	9.0	11.23	10.13	2.23	−1.13	1115.3
	8	9.0	11.64	10.49	2.64	−1.49	1224.4
	9	9.0	11.30	10.41	2.30	−1.41	1206.7
	10	9.0	9.99	9.97	0.99	−0.97	1207.4
	11	8.5	9.43	8.97	0.93	−0.47	1188.9
	12	8.0	8.38	8.16	0.38	−0.16	1211.6
1985	1	8.0	8.35	7.76	0.35	0.24	1286.8
	2	8.0	8.50	8.22	0.50	−0.22	1284.0
	3	8.0	8.58	8.57	0.58	−0.57	1266.8
	4	8.0	8.27	8.0	0.27	0	1258.1
	5	7.5	7.97	7.56	0.47	−0.06	1315.4
	6	7.5	7.53	7.01	0.03	0.49	1335.5
	7	7.5	7.88	7.05	0.38	0.45	1347.5
	8	7.5	7.90	7.18	0.40	0.32	1334.0
	9	7.5	7.92	7.08	0.42	0.42	1328.6
	10	7.5	7.99	7.17	0.49	0.33	1374.3
	11	7.5	8.05	7.20	0.55	0.30	1472.1
	12	7.5	8.27	7.07	0.77	0.43	1546.7
1986	1	7.5	8.14	7.04	0.64	0.46	1571.0
	2	7.5	7.86	7.03	0.36	0.47	1709.1
	3	7.0	7.48	6.59	0.48	0.41	1818.6
	4	7.0	6.99	6.06	−0.01	0.94	1784.0
	5	6.5	6.85	6.15	0.35	0.35	1876.7
	6	6.5	6.90	6.22	0.40	0.28	1885.3

Average
Jan. 1980–June 1986   1.23%   −0.045%

pursuing easier monetary policy, as was the case in the second half of 1982, the Federal Funds' rate was only slightly above the discount rate.

4. From the analysis above, we know that a close examination of the relationships of the three rates (the discount rate, the Federal Funds' rate, and the yield on Treasury Bills) can yield important clues as to the position of the Federal Reserve on monetary policy and the probable trend in the future movement of stock prices.

YIELD CURVE ANALYSIS

The monetary environment at a given point in time can also be examined in terms of the yield curve. A yield curve shows the yield for different maturities of the securities issued by the same entity. Since the U.S. government issues a variety of securities of different maturities (short-term, intermediate-term, and long-term), the yield curve is usually expressed in terms of U.S. government issued securities.

Figure 11-1 shows the different patterns of the yield curve. Yield Curve A is known as an upsloping or "normal" yield curve. It is called "normal" because the risk on longer maturities is usually greater than that of a security with a short-term maturity, and investors demand a higher yield to compensate for the higher risk on longer maturities. Past experience has shown that an upsloping yield curve is favorable to the stock market most of the time.

Figure 11-1
PATTERNS OF THE YIELD CURVE

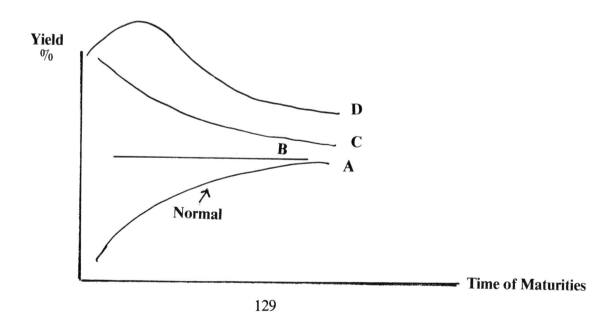

129

Based on his study, Norman Fosback reported that the relationships between the yield curve and future stock prices during the period he studied (1941-1975) were as follows:

Yield Curve	S&P 500 3 Months Later	S&P 500 6 Months Later	S&P 500 1 Year Later
Normal	+ 3%	+ 6%	+11.5%
Abnormal	− 0.5%	− 0.8%	− 0.7%

Yield Curve C, known as a downward sloping yield curve, was usually found in times of high inflation and high interest rates. Yield Curve D, known as a "hump" yield curve, was typically found in periods of monetary stringency. Both types of yield curve, C & D, are usually unfavorable to the stock market, because high inflation, high interest rates, and monetary stringency usually create a difficult environment for business to operate in. As a result, the business community's confidence level is impaired and profit outlooks grow immensely pessimistic. These two factors typically combine to cause a weak stock market.

Yield Curve B, known as a flat yield curve, is usually found in a period of transition; from yield curve A to C, or vice versa. It usually does not last long.

A close examination of the type of yield curve can reveal a lot about the monetary environment the business community is facing at the time and, therefore, provide important clues to future movements in stock prices.

FREE RESERVES AS AN INDICATOR OF MONETARY POLICY AND STOCK MARKET OUTLOOK

The Federal Reserve regulates monetary conditions of the country through influencing the amount of reserves and excess reserves the banks have. The Federal Reserve most frequently uses open market operations (buying and selling government securities in the open market) to achieve its goal of targeting the amount of reserves and excess reserves the banking system should have.

The relationships among reserves, excess reserves and free reserves, can be expressed as follows:

Reserves of the banking system (deposits at Federal Reserve Banks plus vault cash) less reserves required by law for demand and time deposits equals *excess reserves*. Excess reserves less borrowing of banks at the Federal Reserve banks equals *free reserves*.

When the free reserve figure is positive, it means the banks' excess reserves are larger than their borrowing, producing a surplus of reserves. This typically indicates that the Federal Reserve is pursuing an easy monetary policy. Conversely, when the free reserves' amount is a large negative figure (indicating a big reserve deficiency among banks) it usually means the Federal Reserve is pursuing a tight monetary policy.

Table 11-2 shows the amounts of free reserves for the banking system, and the DJIA for the period from January 1980 to May 1986. In 1980 and 1981, free reserves were negative and exceeded one billion most of the time. The stock market was depressed and the DJIA fluctuated within a narrow range of 875 to 950. Beginning in May 1982, the negative free reserves began to shrink sharply and the stock market responded with a substantial rise from 820 DJIA in May 1982 to 1220 DJIA in April 1983. In the second half of 1984, the negative free reserves began to expand again and reached a record level, exceeding seven billion. The stock market finished the year at a level no higher than a year before. Beginning with January 1985, the negative free reserves began to shrink again and in the first five months of 1986 it turned to a positive figure. The stock market responded with upward movement continuously through 1985 and the first 5 months of 1986.

From the data we've just reviewed, it can be readily seen that the *trend* and the *amount* of the free reserves' figure can provide important information on Federal Reserve policy and subsequent movements in stock prices.

Table 11-2
FREE RESERVES OF THE BANKING SYSTEM AND DJIA
Jan. 1980 to May 1986

Date Yr.	Month	Free Reserves (Mil.)		DJIA
1980	1	−	949	875.9
	2	−	1,490	863.1
	3	−	2,383	785.8
	4	−	2,261	817.1
	5	−	845	850.9
	6	−	169	867.9
	7	−	280	935.3
	8	−	357	932.6
	9	−	1,055	932.4
	10	−	1,018	924.5
	11	−	1,201	993.3
	12		1,587	964.0
1981	1	−	913	947.3
	2	−	1,076	974.6
	3	−	624	1003.9
	4	−	1,317	997.8
	5	−	2,023	991.8
	6	−	1,488	976.9
	7	−	1,373	952.3
	8	−	1,137	881.5
	9	−	1,073	850
	10	−	1,032	852.6
	11	−	1,010	889
	12	−	1,041	875
1982	1	−	1,101	871.1
	2	−	1,414	824.4
	3	−	1,254	822.8
	4	−	1,307	848.4
	5	−	745	819.5
	6	−	695	811.9
	7	−	378	808.6
	8	−	199	901.3
	9	−	592	896.3
	10	−	51	991.7
	11	−	177	1039.3
	12	−	197	1046.5
1983	1		46	1075.7
	2	−	122	1112.6
	3	−	415	1130
	4	−	617	1226.2
	5	−	453	1200
	6	−	1,234	1222

Table 11-2 (Cont'd)

Date Yr. Month		Free Reserves (Mil.)	DJIA
1983	7	− 875	1199.2
	8	− 1,127	1216.2
	9	− 943	1233.1
	10	− 332	1225.2
	11	− 383	1276
	12	− 184	1258.6
1984	1	− 102	1220.6
	2	375	1154.6
	3	− 243	1164.9
	4	− 744	1170.8
	5	− 2,411	1104.9
	6	− 2,533	1132.4
	7	− 5,311	1115.3
	8	− 7,338	1224.4
	9	− 6,614	1206.7
	10	− 5,397	1207.4
	11	− 3,924	1188.9
	12	− 2,323	1211.6
1985	1	− 650	1286.8
	2	− 386	1284
	3	− 827	1266.8
	4	− 585	1258.1
	5	− 530	1315.4
	6	− 300	1335.5
	7	− 252	1347.5
	8	− 246	1334
	9	− 623	1328.6
	10	− 434	1374.3
	11	− 813	1472.1
	12	− 260	1546.7
1986	1	341	1571
	2	213	1709.1
	3	135	1818.6
	4	92	1784
	5	43	1876.7

133

Chapter 12

A Composite Judgement On The Probable Market Trend

In the previous eleven chapters we have done the following:

1. Shown the nature and essence of technical analysis and shown why it is often misunderstood, misstated, and misapplied.

2. Explained the Dow Theory; its usefulness and its relationship to modern-day technical analysis.

3. Explained our opinions on how technical analysis should be performed with respect to market conditions.

OUR PROPOSED METHODS
OF ANALYZING MARKET CONDITIONS

The methods we have proposed to analyze market conditions include the following:

1. To identify the market trend (near term, intermediate term, and long term) with the moving average method.

2. To measure the momentum of the market trend.

3. To measure the genuineness of the market trend by the diffusion index of advancing and declining issues on NYSE.

4. To correctly interpret the relationships between the level of volume, volume trend and price changes.

5. To measure market sentiment by:
   a) Price/dividend ratio
   b) Ratio between yield on Treasury Bills and the dividend yield on stocks
   c) The proportion of NYSE stocks above their 10-week moving average
   d) Net subscription of mutual fund by the public
   e) Cash ratio of mutual funds
   f) Short sales ratio of specialists on NYSE
   g) Investment advisory sentiment index

6. To assess the market conditions with additional useful indicators like these:
   a) Degree of speculation in the stock market
   b) Disparity of price movement among these market indexes: DJIA, S&P's 500, Value Line Composite, and NASDAQ OTC Composite
   c) Call volume, Put volume, and their ratio of turnover
   d) Stock Index Futures

7. To measure the monetary environment by:
   a) Relationships among three short-term rates: Discount rate, Federal Funds' rate, and Yield on Treasury Bills
   b) Analysis of yield curve
   c) Trend and level of free reserves.

If the investor or technical analyst follows our procedure to analyze the market conditions as outlined above, we feel he or she is ready to make a judgement on the probable market trend. This judgement should not be difficult to make as our systematic analysis should clearly reveal the internal structure of the market and the state of psychology of market participants.

ORDER OF IMPORTANCE OF THE VARIOUS STEPS OF ANALYSIS OUTLINED ABOVE

Some of our readers may ask us how we rate the relative importance of each step of analysis outlined above. To answer this question, we would say, our preference is to rank the various steps or factors as follows:
1. Volume level and volume trend (Chapters 7 & 8)
2. Market direction, momentum, and diffusion (Chapters 4, 5, 6)

3. Market sentiment (Chapter 9)
4. Other market indicators (Chapter 10)
5. Monetary environment (Chapter 11)

Chapter 13

Selection of Individual Stocks

Those who follow the technical approach to gauge the overall market trend often do not share the same view when selecting an individual stock to buy or sell. Basically, there are three different approaches to selecting an individual stock to buy or sell: the fundamental approach, the technical approach, or a combination of both the fundamental and technical approaches.

SELECTING AN INDIVIDUAL STOCK
TO BUY OR SELL BY THE FUNDAMENTAL APPROACH

First, we have to point out that the investor we are going to be discussing here is a follower of the technical approach for overall market trend, however he prefers to select individual stocks by the fundamental approach.

Since he follows the technical approach for overall market trend, he will be following these two basic technical rules:

1. First, determine the current market trend.
2. Follow the market trend. If the market trend is bullish, be bullish. If the market trend is bearish, be bearish. When the market trend is neutral and indeterminate, do nothing and stay on the sideline.

The fundamental factors each individual investor examines and emphasizes will vary.

However, the most important fundamental factors most investors prefer to look at are these:

1. Quality of management
2. Product lines and research ability
3. New developments within the company
4. Competition
5. Profitability and profit outlook
6. Past record of performance, especially in the last 5 years
7. Possibility of takeover, merger, & acquisition
8. Value of the stock vs. market price

SELECTING AN INDIVIDUAL STOCK TO BUY OR SELL BY THE TECHNICAL APPROACH

Here we deal with an investor who follows the technical approach all the way; both for gauging market trend and for selecting an individual stock to buy or sell.

For this type investor who selects his stock by the technical approach, the basic technical rule is this:

If the current market trend is bullish, (a) buy securities in industry groups which are in an uptrend, and (b) choose securities from those bullish industry groups which are themselves in an uptrend. By uptrend I am, of course, referring to price trend; the industry composite index and the price of the stock.

If the current market trend is bearish, (a) select among groups in a downtrend, and (b) from these bearish industry groups select stocks which themselves are in a downtrend for short-selling.

CHARTING

Charts are important tools to the followers of the technical approach. Technicians usually subscribe to several charting services, and, in addition, do a lot of charting themselves. Charts are of two types: (1) bar charts and (2) point and figure charts. Many technicians use both types.

Bar Charts

Figure 13-1 shows a bar chart of the prices of Avon stock. The bar chart usually shows the daily price range, closing price, and volume of transactions. In this chart, a 50-day moving average of stock prices and a relative strength line of the stock are also included. The relative strength line showing the strength of the stock compared to the market is derived by dividing the price of the stock by the S&P's 500 Composite Index. An upward slope in the line means that the stock is doing relatively better than the S&P's 500.

The bar chart has the advantage of showing price fluctuation in a chronological order and, in addition, the volume of transactions. As we discussed before, the volume of transactions is an important item of information for technical analysis.

Figure 13-1
COMMON STOCK OF AVON PRODUCTS

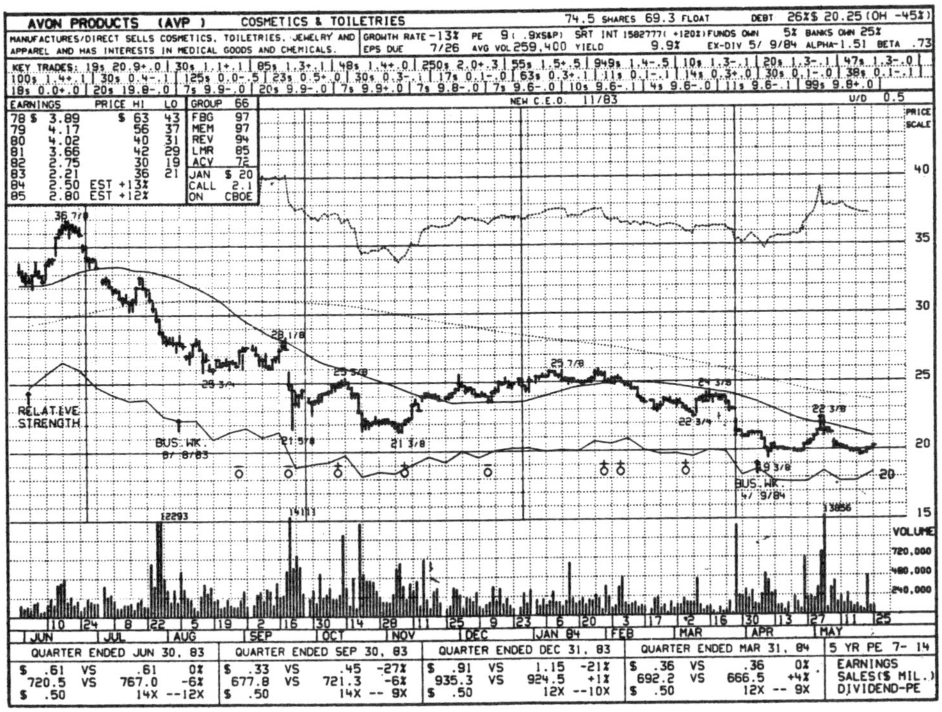

Source: *Daily Graphs,* William O'Neil & Co.

Point and Figure Chart

Figure 13-2 is a point and figure chart for ABC stock. The vertical scale measures the price of the stock. The point and figure chart does not have a time dimension and the horizontal scale is not a time scale. Price is recorded only when the change in price reaches a predetermined magnitude, such as ½, 1, or 2 points. What is most commonly used is a one-point scale. That means the price will not be recorded unless it reaches a round figure such as 1, 2, or 3. Fractional changes are not recorded.

Figure 13-2
THE PRICE OF ABC STOCK

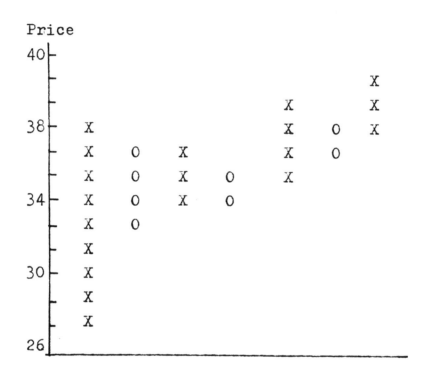

When the price of a stock rises, an X is recorded to indicate the price change. When the price of a stock is going down, an O is recorded to indicate the price change. X's and O's never appear in the same column. Each column represents either an upmove or a downmove; it cannot represent both. When there is a change in price in a different direction (rise after previous declines, or decline after previous increases), the price is recorded in the next column to the right. The first entry on the chart can be labeled by a square or any other sign.

142

For purpose of illustration, let us say the daily closing prices of XYZ stock in the last 20 days were as follows:

$30, 30¼, 31, 31½, 32, 32½, 33, 32¾, 32½, 32, 32¼, 32¾, 33, 33½, 34, 35, 36, 35, 34, 33½

Figure 13-3 shows the resulting point and figure chart of XYZ stock on the basis of these prices.

Figure 13-3
POINT AND FIGURE CHART OF XYZ STOCK

```
    Price
   $36|             X
    35|             X      O
    34|             X      O
    33|      X      X
    32|      X   O
    31|      X
    30|      X
       |_____
```

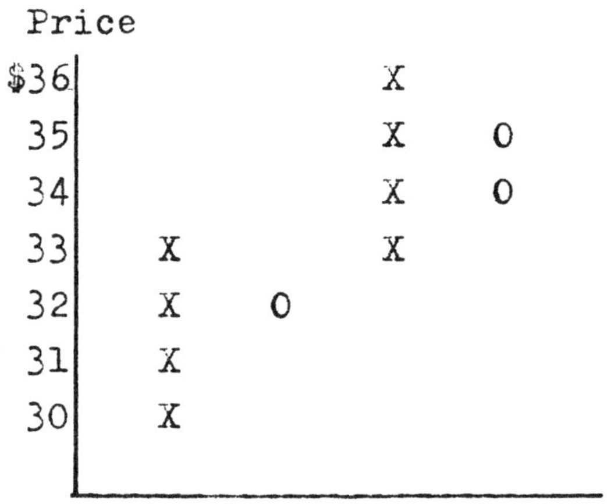

Through eliminating the time scale and small changes, the point and figure chart is designed to compress the recording of price fluctuations of a stock into congested areas so that different chart patterns or formations will emerge clearly.

CHART PATTERNS: TERMS & INTERPRETATION

Technical analysts recognize many different formations or patterns in the charts of stock prices. Some patterns are considered having bullish implications, others bearish, still others are considered basically uncertain and indeterminate for the time being. I will now briefly explain and describe some basic chart patterns.

143

Head & Shoulder Formation

Chartists consider the head-and-shoulders formation one of the most important and reliable of the major *reversal* patterns. It is a bearish pattern. A typical head-and-shoulders formation (shown in Pattern A, Figure 13-4) consists of four basic elements.

1. A strong rally with high volume followed by a minor reaction with less volume.

2. Another high volume advance reaching a higher level than the previous advance followed by a minor reaction at less volume.

3. A third rally but at a much lower volume than the previous advances.

4. Decline of prices from the third rally through the "neck line" drawn across the lows of the previous two reactions.

Triangles or Coils

Technical analysts view triangle or coil formations as patterns of uncertainty. They feel that the odds are in favor of continuing the trend that preceded the formation.

The first portion of Figure 13-5 shows three types of triangles: symmetrical, ascending, and descending. Technical analysts believe that in the case of an ascending triangle, stock price will likely continue to move up, whereas in the case of a descending triangle, the stock price will more likely move downward. The symmetrical triangle, on the other hand, denotes uncertainty.

Support & Resistance Levels

According to technical analysts, the typical pattern of the behavior of investors is as follows: When investors make mistakes and find prices declining after a purchase, they usually grit their teeth and hang on, hoping that they will later be able to get out without a loss. When prices actually start to recover, they usually grasp the first chance to get out at the prices they originally paid. This kind of behavior creates the phenomenon that at certain price levels there will be a considerable increase in supply and the price of a stock will find it difficult to go beyond this level. In the language of the chartist this is called the resistance level. Since more investors buy high than buy low, and there was usually high volume at former highs, the resistance level for a stock tends to establish at its former high.

A support level on the other hand is the level at which a falling stock may expect a considerable increase in demand. The support level is usually established at the level

144

Figure 13-4
TYPICAL GRAPHIC PATTERNS
USED IN TECHNICAL MARKET ANALYSIS

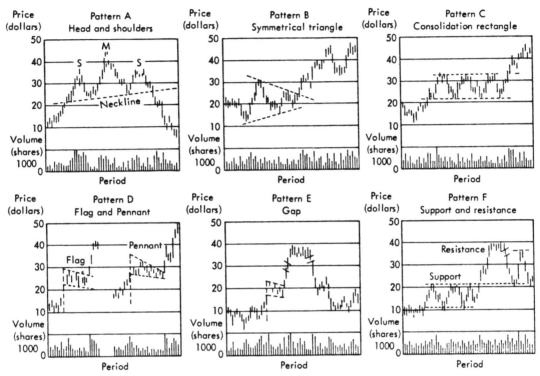

Source: Sidney M. Robbins, *Managing Securities* (Boston: Houghton Mifflin, 1954), p. 502.

Figure 13-5

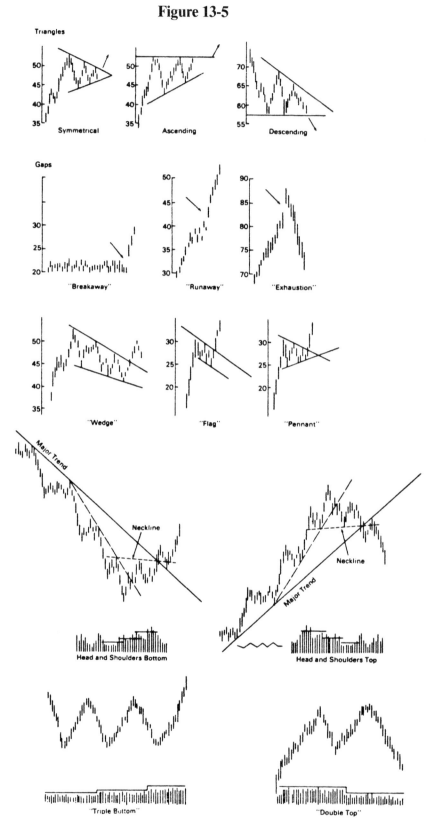

Source: Alan R. Shaw, "Technical Analysis," in Sumner N. Levine, ed., *Financial Analyst's Handbook.* Dow Jones-Irwin, Inc., Homewood, Ill., 1975.

146

from which a stock had previously been rising and where the volume of transactions was heavy. At this support level, a variety of investors may come in to buy the stock. They include (1) those who regretted that they did not buy before when the stock was advancing, (2) short sellers who sold short before and now buy back to take profits, and (3) "value" conscious investors.

Support and resistance levels are shown in pattern F in Figure 13-4

Flags & Pennants

Pattern D in Figure 13-4 shows formations commonly described as flags and pennants. These patterns often appear after a swift, upward movement in prices. These area patterns usually represent consolidation or continuation patterns. In other words, they typically signify a pause after which the previous price trend will likely resume.

Gaps

A gap represents a price range in which no shares change hands. A gap occurs when the lowest price at which a stock is traded on a given day is higher than the highest price of the preceding day. Technicians recognize several types of gaps, such as a breakaway gap, runaway gap, and exhaustion gap. Depending on their location, they may have little significance, or may signify the start of an important move.

Tops & Bottoms

The formation may include two or three tops known as double top or triple top formations. These are bearish formations. On the other hand, if a formation consists of two or three bottoms, the formation is considered bullish. The bottom portion of Figure 13-5 shows a triple bottom and a double top formation.

A formation which includes declining tops as shown in Figure 13-6 (c) is considered bearish. The reverse is a formation of rising bottoms as shown in Figure 13-6 (a), which is considered bullish.

Bullish & Bearish Patterns in Point & Figure Charts

Figure 13-7 shows patterns of four stocks in point and figure charts. The column X, as explained before, is recorded when price is rising. The column O is recorded when price is declining.

Figure 13-6
TOP AND BOTTOM FORMATIONS

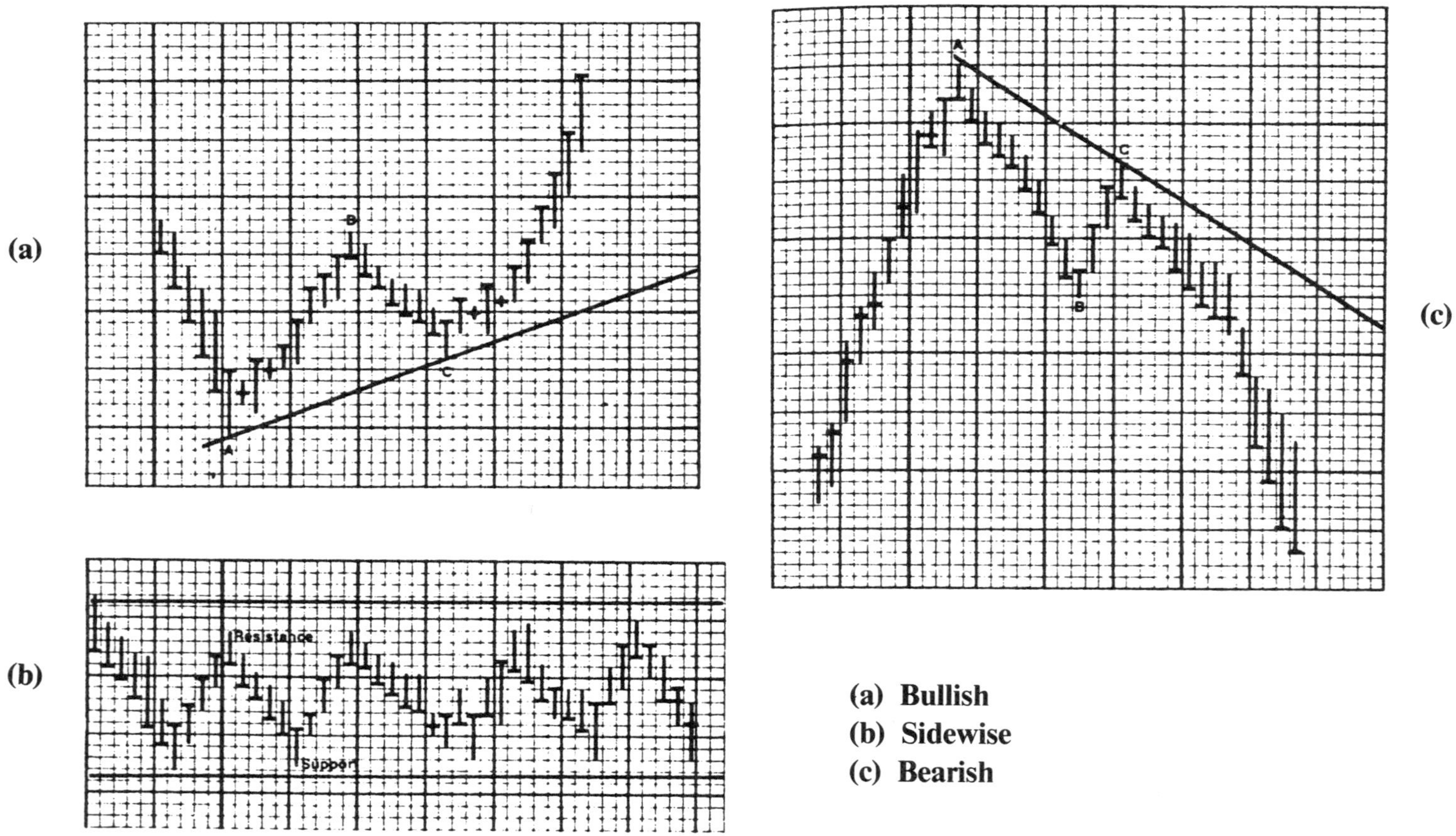

(a) Bullish
(b) Sidewise
(c) Bearish

148

Figure 13-7

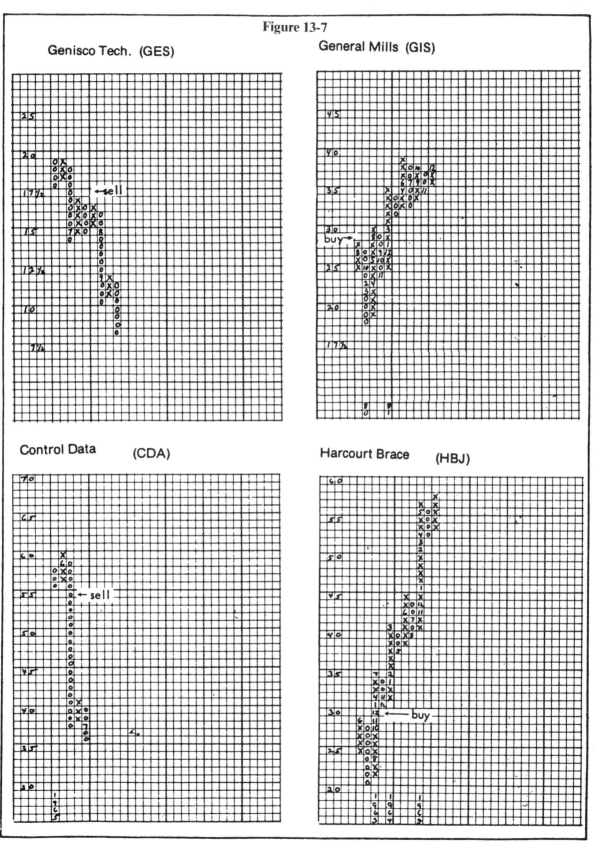

Source: A.W. Cohen, *Op.Cit.,* pp. 45 & 50

149

The sell signal is given when price dipped to a level below the previous low, as shown in the cases of Genisco Tech and Control Data. The numbers in the chart represent the months in which the prices occurred.

When prices rise above the previous top, a buy signal is given, as in the case of General Mills and Harcourt Brace.

Trendline

Figure 13-8 shows trendlines in point and figure charts. The bullish support line, as shown in the second chart, is drawn from the square below the low in a significant downmove. It is drawn at a 45 degree angle. As long as the chart pattern remains above the line, the stock is considered long-term bullish.

The bearish resistance line, shown in the first chart, is drawn from the square above the high and is extended downward to the right at a 45 degree angle. As long as the chart pattern remains below this line, the stock is considered bearish. The few buy signals below this line should have been ignored. In other words, action is taken only when the buy or sell signals given by the pattern of a stock are in agreement with the trendline.

COMMENTS ON THE DIFFERENT APPROACHES TO SELECT INDIVIDUAL STOCKS

A) *Selecting Stock by the Fundamental Approach*

We feel that selecting an individual stock to buy or sell does not have to be on the same basis as the gauging of the market trend. There is no logical reason why technical analysis for the overall market trend cannot be combined with the selection of an individual stock using fundamental analysis. However, as we have pointed out earlier, in order to be logical the investor who uses technical analysis to gauge market trend, first has to determine the market trend and then must select the individual stock to go with the market trend. In a bull market he should be long in stocks with appreciation potential. Conversely, in a bear market he should be short in stocks deemed to be weak fundamentally.

B) *Selecting Stock by the Technical Approach*

From our previous discussion it should be clear that we have no objection to the

Figure 13-8

THE BEARISH RESISTANCE LINE

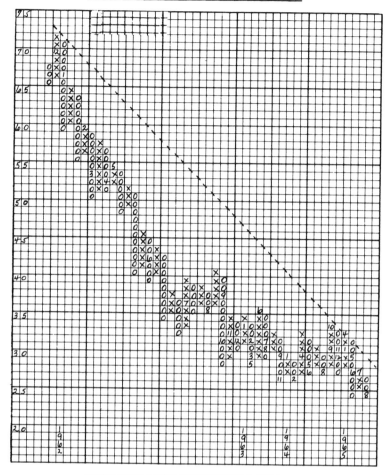

THE BULLISH SUPPORT LINE

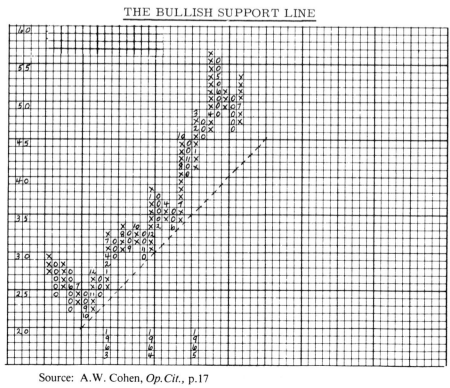

Source: A.W. Cohen, *Op.Cit.,* p.17

151

investor using the technical approach for gauging the market trend as well as for selecting the individual stock. However, since he will be basing his selection on the chart pattern of the stock, he should know that he deals with *probabilities.* The strong pattern of a stock in a bull market may originate from manipulation, rumor, or other transient factors which can easily and quickly turn against the investor. Therefore, in dealing with probabilities he needs to place stop orders to limit his possible loss. He should also observe the principle of diversification.

The concepts we discussed before in relation to market analysis such as rate of change, volume level, volume trend, and volume momentum, apply also to the selection of an individual stock. The investor can use these concepts to supplement the use of chart patterns in selecting individual stocks.

C) *Selecting Stock by Combined Approach of Referring To Both Fundamental Factors and Chart Patterns of Stocks*

The investor in this case wants to select stocks on the basis of both fundamental and technical factors. He wants to check the company in terms of fundamental factors as an added safeguard in his selection of stocks based on technical chart patterns. Certainly, we are not against this more conservative approach in stock selection. As a matter of fact, we like the idea of checking both technical and fundamental factors in selecting a stock for purchase or sale. Since the investor embraces the technical approach for his overall market analysis, he, like others following different approaches, needs to observe the basic principle of determining the market trend first and then implementing stock selection to go with the market trend.

Chapter 14

Strategic Use of
Fundamental Factors

Since technical analysis is very different from fundamental analysis, many investors and analysts who follow the technical approach believe that the fundamental factors should not be considered because they would not add anything positive to the analysis. Others go a step further and argue that consideration of fundamental factors would confuse investors using the technical approach and would, in fact, be harmful to investment performance. Our views are different and we will examine the question carefully in this next section.

**WHY DO INVESTORS FOLLOWING THE TECHNICAL APPROACH
ALSO NEED TO KEEP ABREAST OF
FUNDAMENTAL FACTORS PREVAILING AT THE TIME?**

The five main reasons are as follows:

1. It's a fact that many successful investors and traders who claim they are believers and followers of the technical approach are also very knowledgeable in fundamental factors.
2. Many times investment decisions on the surface are attributable to technical factors. However, a more careful analysis often reveals that the decision-maker is also aware of the fundamental factors involved at the time.

3. Investing is an art as well as a science. A successful investor or trader needs to be skillful in mapping both investment strategy and tactics. Strategy is all-embracing and deals with a longer-term perspective. Fundamental factors are important in devising proper strategy. Tactics, on the other hand, relate action to specific circumstances and time. Technical analysis is helpful in this area.

4. As we mentioned earlier (in Chapter 11) nowadays most technical analysts include interest rates and monetary policy as technical indicators. Theoretically, interest rates and monetary policy are fundamental factors which cause changes in security prices and, therefore, belong to the domain of the fundamental approach. In other words, the technical analysis most analysts follow today is already a mixed approach, though the fundamental factors are probably given less weight than the technical factors.

5. The business cycle is closely related to the stock market cycle. A knowledge of the fundamental factors prevailing at the time can help gauge the stage of the business cycle and, therefore, the potentials in the stock market.

EMPIRICAL EVIDENCE OF THE BUSINESS CYCLE AND THE STOCK MARKET CYCLE

Figure 14-1 shows stock prices as measured by S&P's 500 since 1950. The shaded areas represent recessions. They were: 1953-54, 1957-58, 1960, 1970, 1974, 1980, and 1981-82. A close examination of the chart and other materials revealed the following:

1. Major market lows occurred in 1953, 1957, 1960, 1962, 1966, 1970, 1974, 1978, 1980, and 1984.
2. Most major market lows happened in recession years.
3. A long business cycle (over 4 years in length) usually contained 2 stock market cycles.
4. A short business cycle (less than 3 years in length) usually contained one stock market cycle.
5. The up-phase of a stock market cycle usually lasts 2 years, or slightly less.

THE MAIN FEATURES OF A MAJOR MARKET CYCLE

In Figure 14-2 you will see the main features of a stock market cycle outlined. There

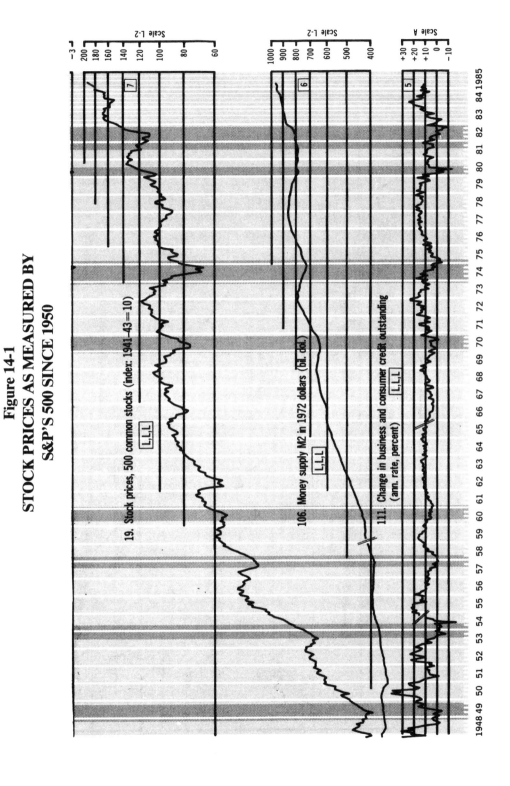

Figure 14-1
STOCK PRICES AS MEASURED BY
S&P'S 500 SINCE 1950

19. Stock prices, 500 common stocks (index: 1941-43=10)

106. Money supply M2 in 1972 dollars (bil. dol.)

111. Change in business and consumer credit outstanding (ann. rate, percent)

Figure 14-2
THE TYPICAL PATTERN OF A STOCK MARKET CYCLE,
CONTAINING TWO INTERMEDIATE CYCLES

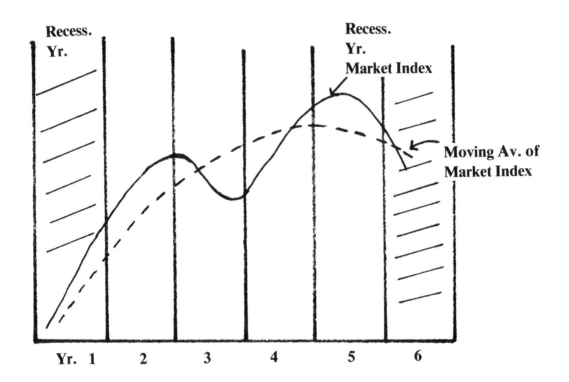

you'll see the typical pattern of a stock market cycle, containing two intermediate cycles. The shaded areas represent recessions. The major cycle is represented by a dotted curve which is a moving average of some length of a stock index (like DJIA or S&P's 500). The main features of this hypothetical market cycle are these:

1. Being a leading indicator of general business, stock prices began to recover in year 1 when the recession was still in progress. In year 5, stock prices began to decline when general business was still good.

2. The length of the market cycle was assumed to be 5 years, the same length as the business cycle.

3. The upmove in stock prices from the recession lasted about 2 years. In the third year, a correction took place retracting about 1/3 of the previous upmove.

4. In the 4th year a resumption of the upmove began and most likely carried to the next year.

5. In the latter part of the 5th year, stock prices began to move down in anticipation of a recession in general business in the following year.

THE FEATURES OF A MINOR MARKET CYCLE

If the business recovery was weak and lasted three years or less, then the stock market cycle would be most likely also of a minor magnitude. The features of this minor market cycle would most likely include these:

1. The recovery in stock prices from recession would be most likely mild.

2. There will be periods of minor reactions and sidewise movements in stock prices.

3. In the third year, stock prices would begin to decline in anticipation of a downturn in general business.

The experience of the stock market during 1971-1973 resembled very closely what we described above.

FACTORS AFFECTING THE BUSINESS CYCLE

The discussions above would indicate that the knowledge of factors affecting the business cycle and the ability to gauge its progress should be very helpful to investors in setting up investment strategy and in gauging the potentials of the stock market at the time.

The fundamental factors affecting the business cycle are these:

1. Rate of inflation
2. Level of interest rates
3. Monetary policy of the Federal Reserve
4. Prospect of profits and profit margin in the eyes of businessmen
5. Balance or imbalance in the major areas of the economy:
   a) Federal budget
   b) Balance of payments
   c) External value of the dollar vs. balance of payments
   d) The growth pattern of the major sectors of the economy: manufacturing, agriculture, mining and servicing.

Chapter 15

The Individual Investor
And Technical Analysis—A Summary

That completes our presentation of what I believe to be an objective view of technical analysis. To summarize:

1. Technical analysis is market analysis. If it is properly performed, it can help the investor to gauge the market trend with a high degree of success.

2. The methods we proposed to systematically analyze market conditions include the following steps:

    a) To identify the market trend by the moving average method

    b) To measure the genuineness of the market trend

    c) To measure the strength and the momentum of the market trend

    d) To correctly interpret the relationships between level of volume, volume trend and price changes

    e) To measure market sentiment

    f) To assess several selected useful indicators

    g) To measure the monetary environment

    h) To make a composite judgement of the most likely future market trend

3. The cardinal rule of technical analysis is to determine market trend first and then select individual stocks to go with the trend. Those who follow the technical approach should always observe this rule.

4. Investors following the technical approach differ in ways of selecting individual stocks. Some go by chart patterns. Others rely on fundamental factors. Still others rely

on both technical and fundamental factors. While we are not opposed to any approach, we do prefer the combined approach.

5. While the technical approach is very useful to professional traders, in our view it offers only a limited advantage to the general public for trading purposes. The reasons are these:

a) They hold jobs away from the market. They cannot take advantage of fast changing developments in the market.

b) Most of them do not have enough knowledge of technical market analysis. Moreover, they cannot afford to subscribe to the many different technical market advisory and chart services.

c) Unlike most professional traders, the general public does not strictly follow trading rules.

6. Since the technical approach emphasizes the determination of the current market trend, the approach is useful to the general public in timing their purchases and sales. It's also useful, from time to time, in deciding on a possible modification in portfolio mix among bonds, stocks and money market funds.

7. Many experienced traders are knowledgeable in both fundamental and technical approaches. However, since they are basically interested in taking advantage of short swings in stock prices, they lean most heavily on the technical approach. In our view, a knowledge of the fundamental factors affecting the business cycle, and a rough estimate of the current stage of the business cycle, can help both traders and non-traders in their investment decisions.

8. Though we prefer to identify the market trend by the moving average method, we find the tenets of the Dow Theory still valid and useful.

Bibliography

Cohen, A. W., *Point and Figure,* Chartcraft, Inc., Larchmont, N.Y., 1982.

Drew, Garfield A., *New Methods for Profit in the Stock Market,* Fraser Publishing Co., Wells, Vermont, 1966.

Edwards, Robert D. and Magee, John, *Technical Analysis of Stock Trends,* Springfield Massachusetts, John Magee, 1966.

Fosback, Norman G., *Stock Market Logic,* The Institute of Econometric Research, Fort Lauderdale, Florida, 1976.

Gordon, William, *Stock Market Indicators,* Investors' Press, Inc., Palisades, N.J., 1968.

Granville, Joseph E., *A Strategy of Daily Stock Market Timing for Maximum Profits,* Prentice-Hall, Englewood Cliffs, N.J., 1960.

Hamilton, William P., *The Stock Market Barometer,* Harper & Bros., N.Y., 1932.

Huang, Stanley S.C., *A New Technical Approach to Stock Market Timing,* Investors Intelligence, Larchmont, N.Y., 1973.

Indicator Digest's New Directory of Indicators, Indicator Digest Group, Inc., Palisades Park, N.J., 1984.

Investors Intelligence, Inc., *The New Encyclopedia of Stock Market Techniques,* 1985.

Jiler, William L., *How Charts Can Help You in the Stock Market,* Trendline, Inc., N.Y., 1972.

Krow, Harvey A., *Stock Market Behavior,* Random House, N.Y., 1969.

Levy, Robert A., *The Relative Strength Concept of Common Stock Price Forecasting,* Investors Intelligence, Inc., Larchmont, N.Y., 1968.

Neill, Humphrey B., *The Art of Contrary Thinking,* The Caxton Printers, Ltd., Caldwell, Idaho, 1954.

Pring, Martin J., *Technical Analysis Explained,* McGraw-Hill Book Co., N.Y., 1980.

Rhea, Robert, *Dow Theory,* Barron's, N.Y., 1932.

Schabacker, Richard W., *Stock Market Theory and Practice,* Forbes Publishing Co., N.Y., 1930.

Schultz, Harry D. and Coslow, Samson (Editors), *A Treasury of Wall Street Wisdom,* Investors' Press, Inc., Palisades Park, N.J., 1966.

Stone and Mead, Inc., *Long-Term Technical Trends,* current issue, Boston, Massachusetts.

Zweig, Martin E., *Winning on Wall Street,* Warner Books, N.Y., 1986.